TABLE OF CONTENTS

Your Assignment Is
Any Problem God
Created You To Solve
On The Earth.

-MIKE MURDOCK

1

THE UNCOMMON FATHER EMBRACES HIS FAMILY AS HIS DIVINE ASSIGNMENT ON THE EARTH.

The Family Is Not An Experiment.
The Family is a God-idea.
The Uncommon Father knows this and treasures his family as his Divine Assignment as a Golden Gift from God.

1.   The Family Is The Divine Design For The Celebration Of Love. It is the Divine Plan for the reproduction of the human race. It was not a human idea evolving from the imagination of a lonely man, Adam. It is the earthly picture of the spiritual union between the Church and Jesus.

God planned the Family.

God wants *you* to place *great* value on *your* Family.

2.   The Family Was More Than Moral Protection From The Temptation Of Immorality. Other women did not yet exist.

3.   The Family Was More Than A Shield From Potential Enemies. *No enemy had yet appeared.* Before satan ever revealed himself, emerged, God said, "...It is not good that man should be alone;" (Genesis 2:18).

4. The Family Was Not A Substitution For Work, Career Or A Productive Life. It was intended to be the Miracle of Completion, resolving the emotional emptiness in man.

▶ *Celebrate your Family.*

▶ *Protect your Family.*

▶ *Make your Family your Priority Focus.*

▶ *Your Family Is Your Divine Assignment.*

Your Assignment is to be accepted, not altered.

You cannot improve on a Divine instruction!

You Cannot Afford The Tragedies Of An Ignored Instruction. You cannot alter God's words to you without paying a terrible price.

Achan is a sad but enlightening story in the Old Testament. When the children of Israel took Jericho, they were forbidden to keep any of the spoils of war. Achan disobeyed. His sin was discovered when the army went out to take the city of Ai, but failed miserably. When Joshua went before the Lord to ask *why* He had abandoned His people, God told him that it was because one of them had disobeyed His orders. God then revealed to Joshua that it was Achan. The rest is a tragic picture. Joshua had him stoned to death along with his whole family and all his livestock. (Read Joshua 7:1-26 for the full story.)

When You Get The Wrong People Out Of Your Life, The Wrong Things Stop Happening.

Jonah is another classic example. God told him to go to Nineveh. He went to Tarshish instead. God then scheduled three torturous days in the bottom of a huge fish. I call this "Whale University!" He was finally vomited up. It is the miserable story of a disobedient man of God.

There is another important truth here. Note that the sailors who were carrying a rebellious man of God on their ship experienced the horrible frightening storm of the sea. When they threw Jonah overboard, the storm subsided.

> ▶ What You Fail To *Destroy* Will Eventually *Destroy* You.

King Saul was instructed to kill all of the Amalekites, enemies of God. Saul altered the instructions. He permitted King Agag to live. It is noteworthy that later on when a man took the credit for killing Saul, it was an Amalekite.

> ▶ What You Fail To *Master* Will Eventually *Master* You.

> ▶ What You Fail To *Conquer* Will Eventually *Conquer* You.

Judas refused to solve a *greed* problem. Samson refused to solve a *lust* problem. In the end, they were both destroyed.

Do Not Attempt To Alter Your Assignment. *Just do it.*

Remember: *Your Assignment Is To Be Accepted, Not Altered.*

The Uncommon Father knows that he is a reward to his family. Moses was needed as a leader to the children of Israel. He was their *reward*. David was needed by the Israelites to defeat Goliath. He was a *reward* to King Saul as well, when he defeated Goliath and routed the Philistines.

Naomi needed a caretaker. Ruth was a reward for her, and so loyal that her devotion was recorded in the Scriptures for people to read of throughout generations.

The Jews would have been destroyed except for Esther. Esther was their answer, their solution, their *reward.*

Pharaoh desperately needed someone to interpret his dream. Joseph was a *reward* to him and subsequently to the people of Egypt.

Famine would have destroyed the Egyptians. Joseph was *their* reward because he interpreted the message from God through the dream of Pharaoh.

Everything God Created Is A Reward To Somebody. Think about this. It is very important that you as a Father grasp *your* significance and value.

Your *patience* is a reward for somebody that others would not tolerate. Your *words* will motivate someone incapable of seeing what you see. It may be the mental, emotional or spiritual qualities God has developed within you, *but somebody desperately needs you today.*

Father, God planned you. Nobody else can be like you. *Nobody else* can do what you do. You are unlike anyone else on earth. You are Uncommon! Grasp this. Embrace it. God is not a duplicator. He is a Creator. You are absolutely perfect and genetically accurate for *solving a specific problem* for somebody on earth.

Somebody Needs Exactly What You Have Been Given By God. Somebody is hungry and thirsty for *your* presence. Somebody will starve *without you* entering their life. Someone is literally dying, emotionally, mentally or spiritually, *waiting* *for you* to come along and rescue them. Somebody has been lying awake at night praying that God would send you into their life.

You are their reward.

Does everybody need you? Of course not. It is important that you recognize that some people do not really need you. You are *not* their answer. You are *not* their solution. Do not take offense at this. God has somebody else planned for them.

You are not needed *everywhere.* You are only needed at a specific *place,* at a specific *time* and for a specific *person.*

Your family *qualifies* for your entrance into their life. They may not initially see you as being their reward, but you really are. You are *exactly* what God has ordered for their life.

Meditate on this truth. *Taste* it. *Feel* it. *Believe* it. Become...The *Uncommon* Father!

There Are 3 Important Keys To Remember Here

1. God Has Qualified You To Be The Perfect Solution For Your Family.

2. It Is The Responsibility Of Your Family To Discern Your Assignment To Them.

The Pharisees did not discern that Jesus was assigned to them, but Zacchaeus did, and the relationship was born. Even Pharaoh of Egypt, an unbeliever, discerned that Joseph was the answer to his dream and dilemma. Thousands were sick and blind, but one cried out, "Jesus, Thou Son of David, have mercy on me" (see Mark 10:47).

3. When You Fully Embrace The Assignment To Your Family, You Will Experience Great Peace, Fulfillment, Provision And A Special Grace For This Assignment.

You must determine and know well the anointing and calling on your own life. Stand strong, and stay linked to the Holy Spirit in total dependency, and God will direct you.

Look for opportunities to heal, strengthen and bless your family. Do good every time it is possible. "Withhold not good from them to whom it is due, when it is in the power of thine hand to do it" (Proverbs 3:27).

You are truly a gift and reward to those *to whom you are assigned...*your family.

Remember: *You Are A Reward To Someone.*

Let's Pray Together...

"Holy Spirit, You chose me for my Assignment, my family. Empower me to be an Uncommon Father. I reject mediocrity, average and normal. You have anointed me to walk, live and make supernatural decisions. In Jesus' name. Amen."

2

THE UNCOMMON FATHER DISCERNS THAT SATAN IS THE ENEMY TO HIS HOME.

Your Home Has An Enemy.

Anything Good Is Despised By Everything Evil. So, you have an invisible adversary.

The Uncommon Father must have a supernatural awareness of his enemy...and depend on God's Wisdom for discerning.

1. Every Gift From God Will Be Contested By Satan. The Holy Spirit recorded a fascinating conversation between God and satan... regarding the blessings of Job. Satan was wroth and infuriated that the pleasure and prosperity of Job had become one of the great pleasures and delights of God, his Provider.

What Pleasures You Angers Satan.

2. Satan Wants To Place Thorns In Your Nest...Your Home. He continually observes the plans of God. Anything receiving the attention of God instantly receives the attention of hell. Be alert.

3. Satan Wants To Be The Third Party In Your Home. He wants to agitate...anger... disappoint. Using your own weaknesses, he inspires unrealistic expectations, diverts your focus from servanthood to self-absorption. He fuels your imagination through television and relationships...until the Presence of God dissipates and ceases to be the primary goal of your home.

4. Continuously Scan Your Environment For An Adversarial Entry. Look for any symptom of satanic strategy. Listen for the sounds of discontent, fear, pain.

Fight to keep keenly aware of satanic inroads. *Become the Watchman over your home.*

❧ **3** ❧

THE UNCOMMON FATHER ANTICIPATES AND RESISTS ANYONE ATTEMPTING TO INJECT DOUBT, FEAR OR STRIFE INTO HIS HOME ENVIRONMENT.

Thoughts Have Presence.

You can walk into a home and sense confusion, bitterness, doubt, jealousy or joy. The attitude, energy, enthusiasm or sorrow of the human spirit is contagious.

One lady shared an interesting discovery with me. When a close friend went on her vacation, her relationship with her family instantly improved. In fact, it seemed strife-free...until her friend returned. Then, the contention and friction reappeared. Reluctantly but firmly, she accepted that evil communications corrupt good manners. **Each Friendship Is An Ingredient That Changes The Equation Of Your Life.**

One husband noted that certain television shows nurtured an unsettling *sexual restlessness* within him. He was *comparing* his wife with the sensuality of the performers.

The Role Of Every Parent
Is To Decide
Who Qualifies
To Be An Influence
On Their Child.

-MIKE MURDOCK

A young wife identified the timing of unexplainable jealousy toward her husband...after watching her favorite soap opera on television.

Every emotion has a birthplace, a beginning.

Stay watchful, vigilant and sensitive to any changes in the environment of your home or inner life.

Never Complain About
What You Permit.

-MIKE MURDOCK

≈ 4 ≈

THE UNCOMMON FATHER DECIDES THE HEROES, KNOWLEDGE AND INFLUENCES HIS FAMILY NEEDS.

Your Home Is Your Palace, Father!

1. Decide The Climate That Dominates Your House. Remember these factors: words permitted, disorder allowed, colors of the walls, television programs, choice of music, scented candles.

2. Carefully Design A Specific Strategy That Creates That Environment. My mother was a master at it. She sculptured the *music* we heard...the instruments of piano, accordion, guitar. She carefully selected the *biographies* of Uncommon Achievers who would become our childhood heroes. She selected every book in our library.

3. Invest Significant Time In Visualizing The Perfect Atmosphere. What is The Dream Environment...that you want to be in your home? Find pictures in magazines or books that clarify this inner photograph.

4. Create Your Library List Of Heroes. Collect books on them. Discuss those whose greatness affected millions. Who are the Top Ten

Champions of Greatness that you are teaching your children to admire?

5. Choose Four Family Conferences To Attend Annually. This *Preventive* Planning... accesses Mentorship that will prevent the decay of your family...every 90 days.

6. Use The Walls Of Your Home To Announce The Future You Are Pursuing.

What You See Determines What You Desire.

What You Keep Seeing You Begin To Believe.

RECOMMENDED FOR YOUR WISDOM LIBRARY:
TS-37 31 Secrets Of The Uncommon Mentor (6 tapes/$30)
Order Today! www.TheWisdomCenter.tv

≈ 5 ≈

THE UNCOMMON FATHER CAREFULLY CHOOSES A HOME CHURCH THAT REFLECTS HIS BELIEFS.

———————●———————

Your Church Reveals Your Priorities.

Some churches are chosen because they are conveniently close. Some churches are chosen because they are publicized and well-known.

1. **Recognize The Pastor Whose Counsel Is From The Heart Of The Holy Spirit.** You should choose a pastor who is a true spiritual Mentor, unleashing a new passion for The Word of God.

2. **Make Your Church The Center Of Your Activities, Interest And Time.** Limit career participation...school games...or whatever. But, always, make your Spiritual Life the first Priority of your time and attention.

3. **Create A List Of Your Personal Spiritual Concerns.** This includes the basic foundation truths that you view important and vital.

4. **Discern What Involvement And Time The Holy Spirit Wants You To Invest Into Your Church Family And Goals.** You may want to

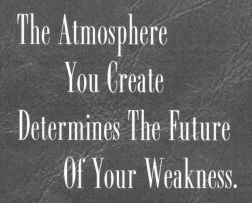

The Atmosphere
You Create
Determines The Future
Of Your Weakness.

-MIKE MURDOCK

teach, sing in the choir or host a monthly Scriptural Success Breakfast for the business persons in your church.

Your church should be your Mentorship Center. Never trivialize the decision that determines the quality of your life.

The Quality Of
Your Questions
Reveal The Quality
Of Your Caring.

-*MIKE MURDOCK*

❧ 6 ❧

THE UNCOMMON FATHER ASKS QUESTIONS THAT REVEAL HIS RESPECT FOR THE OPINIONS OF HIS FAMILY.

Home Is Access.

The opinions, observations and discoveries of others in your family can unlock a new level of understanding. Invest time to listen, learn and evaluate the suggestions, needs and desires of your mate and children.

1. **Your Family Are Your Personal Confidantes.** They may become your best friends. Their counsel is critical.

2. **Your Passion To Pleasure Is Contagious.** When you master the Art of Pleasure... toward your family...you will unleash an indescribable influence on your environment.

3. **Your Questions Reveal Your Caring.** Create a personal list of questions you want answered about the pain, memories, dreams and fears of your family.

4. **Your Willingness To Listen Becomes A Portrait Of Your Humility.** Listen long enough for the hidden emotions to be expressed. Listen carefully enough to collect sufficient understanding. Listen accurately...so you can assess the true needs

Reaching
Proves
Caring!

-MIKE MURDOCK

of your family...that nobody else has been able to meet.

5. The Questions You Ask Decide The Answers You Discover.

You Have No Right To Anything You Have Not Pursued.

Loyalty
Is The Proof
Of Character.

-MIKE MURDOCK

7

THE UNCOMMON FATHER FOCUSES ON THE FAVORABLE QUALITIES OF HIS FAMILY THAT DISTINGUISH THEM FROM OTHERS.

Your Family Is Unlike Anyone Else.

Some qualities are the magnets that keep you together. Additional great qualities developed into a current that swiftly moved you into intimacy, confidentiality, commitment...and the Divine Covenant of The Home.

1. Remember Your Chosen Focus Is The World You Have Decided To Create For Yourself. *Your Focus Will Decide Your Feelings.* When you focus on the admirable differences of your family, you will instantly generate hope, warmth and cheerfulness.

2. List Seven Favorable Qualities Of Your Mate And Family Members. Document them in your Private Journal. Do not trivialize any of them. If you can list more, do so. If these qualities were missing, your life would certainly become painful...in a day.

3. Verbalize Your Recognition Of Those Qualities To Your Family Members And

Focus Magnifies.

-MIKE MURDOCK

Others. This births a climate of acceptance and caring where the Seeds of Love and Loyalty can grow.

 4. Expect The Divine Law Of Sowing And Reaping To Work In Your Favor. Your Seeds of Love will grow.

 Your Focus Always Decides Your Feelings.

Nothing Is Ever
As Bad As It
First Appears.

-MIKE MURDOCK

❦ 8 ❦

THE UNCOMMON FATHER USES THE IRRITATING TRAITS OF HIS FAMILY AS AN OPPORTUNITY TO HEAL.

Pain Talks.

View every moment of irritation, pain and stress as a School of Discovery. Words are pictures of information. Conversations impart knowledge. Every human hurts. Somewhere. Some strive to escape their inner pain through their work... alcohol...illicit sex...drugs or even anger. So when the behavior of your family agitates or even infuriates you, it is Learning Time. Time to *listen* and *learn*. It is an opportunity to heal.

My dear friend, Pastor Sherman Owens says to listen to happy voices for encouragement. But, listen to the *unhappy* voices for *ideas* and information!

1. Learn About The Expectations Of Your Family. Are they unrealistic? Were they unexpressed or unknown until this confrontation? Anger is usually disappointment.

2. Listen For The Sounds Of Disappointment. Often, during quarrels and heated conversations, suddenly memories of child-hood abuse or disappointment in a parent reappear.

3.   Focus Your Prayers For The Healing Of Your Family.   One mother went into a rage when her family members were late coming home from work or school. She imagined rejection and rebellion. The uncontrollable rage revealed root insecurity and a sense of insignificance and unworthiness. This revelation forever changed the prayer focus of her family. They became her faithful Intercessors.

Two Are Always Better Than One.

❦ 9 ❧

THE UNCOMMON FATHER ESTABLISHES A SPECIFIC MORNING ROUTINE FOR HIS FAMILY ALTAR.

Reaching Proves Humility.

*Prayer is reaching...*for Divine assistance. Nothing impresses the heart of The Father more. *Prayer involves God in your family.* "And ye shall seek Me, and find Me, when ye shall search for Me with all your heart. And I will be found of you, saith the Lord:" (Jeremiah 29:13,14).

The habit of prayer prevailed in my home as a boy. Father insisted on it. Twice a day. Morning and night.

Successful Fathers Do Daily What Unsuccessful Fathers Do Occasionally.

1. Embrace Prayer As The Divine Instrument For Healing. "...I have heard thy prayer, I have seen thy tears: behold, I will heal thee:" (2 Kings 20:5)

2. Establish A Specific Time To Pray Together Each Morning. Keep it brief. Though uncomfortable at first, the awkwardness dissolves when ritualized...as a part of your morning routine.

3. Set Aside A Specific Place Or Room

What You Do Daily
Determines
What You Become
Permanently.

-MIKE MURDOCK

For This Divine Appointment Each Morning With The Holy Spirit. I have sanctified my special room as...The Secret Place. Name your place whatever inspires you...The Upper Room... The War Room...My Garden of Prayer...or whatever makes it meaningful to *you*.

4. **Create A Basic Plan And Pattern For Prayer.** Keep a Pictorial Prayer Book. List the names, needs and pictures for your focus. Keep a list of scriptures for Confession and Faith-building.

The Secret Of Your Success Is Always Hidden In Your Daily Routine.

5. **Nurture The Memory Of A Praying Father In The Minds Of Your Children.** What they *see* you do will last forever in their minds, much longer than what they hear you say.

Let's Pray Together...
"Holy Spirit, motivate me to demonstrate my confidence in the power of prayer...to my children. Enable me to birth the heart of an intercessor. In Jesus' name. Amen."

An Uncontested Adversary
Always Flourishes.

-MIKE MURDOCK

⚙ 10 ⚙

THE UNCOMMON FATHER EXERCISES HIS SPIRITUAL AUTHORITY DURING ANY DEMONIC ATTACK.

Every Father Has An Invisible Enemy.

Satan despises the power of women on the earth. The Garden of Eden reveals this.

1. Remember Everything Good Is Despised By Everything Evil. The book of Job documents this when satan complained to God about the loyalty of Job.

2. Identify The Person Or Method Satan Uses To Introduce Anger, Agitation Or Contention. Is it a television show that stirs up lust, jealousy, envy or fear? Is there a *relationship* that feeds conflict and *unrest* in your family? Pinpoint it honestly...then address it in the privacy of your prayer life.

3. Accept The Holy Spirit As The Power Source That Honors Your Position Of Authority Over Evil Influences. Any Uncontested Enemy Will Flourish. "Ye are of God, little children, and have overcome them: because greater is He that is in you, than he that is in the world" (1 John 4:4).

4. Dominate Your Home Environment Daily With Power Praying. Walk through your home singing, worshipping and confessing the Word of God aloud. "Speaking to yourselves in psalms and hymns and spiritual songs, singing...to the Lord;" (Ephesians 5:19).

Let's Pray Together...
"Holy Spirit, You are welcome in this home. Nothing will be permitted that offends You.
We bind and remove every evil spirit from this home. In the name of Jesus. Amen."

⪢ 11 ⪢

THE UNCOMMON FATHER STAYS DISCREET ABOUT FAMILY PROBLEMS.

Talk Magnifies Everything.

When you talk about your problems to everyone, you perpetuate the memory of them. It positions you as a victim...and delays any efforts for recovery.

Every Father decides what his family remembers most. Your legacy is decided subconsciously. *Let wrong events die.*

1. **Bad News Is Remembered Longer Than Good News.** So, years after you have resolved a conflict, others will continue to focus on it.

2. **The Wise Never Discuss Their Problems With Someone Incapable Of Solving Them.** Your chosen confidante should be competent and discreet...with a proven history of competent counsel. Not your nine-year-old child.

3. **Someone You Are Trusting Is Trusting Someone Else You Would Not**. Who have your friends chosen to trust? Whose advice and companionship do they pursue?

4. **Problem-Talk Portrays You As The Victim, Not The Overcomer.** Nobody backs

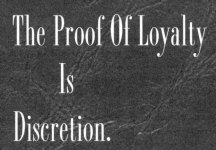

The Proof Of Loyalty
Is
Discretion.

-MIKE MURDOCK

losers. When Job lost everything, everyone avoided him. It was only when God doubled his blessings that others returned to participate in his life by giving him gifts. Harness your mouth, thoughts and focus.

Silence Can Never Be Misquoted.

Let's Pray Together...

"Holy Spirit, Your words only will come through my mouth today. I will only speak words of life, peace and victory. My family will hear only glorious and happy reports through my lips today. I am an Uncommon Father...whose words are holy, righteous and victorious! In Jesus' name. Amen."

Whatever Is Missing
In Your Life Is
Something You Have
Not Yet Truly Valued.

-MIKE MURDOCK

≈ **12** ≈

THE UNCOMMON FATHER INVESTS TIME IN DISCOVERING THE GOALS, DREAMS, GIFTS AND POTENTIAL OF HIS FAMILY.

━━━━━►≫•◦•≪◄━━━━━

Diamonds Are Deep In The Earth.
Gold requires unending search and scrutiny.
The Uncommon Father sees what others are too busy to discern.

1. Your Family Is The Gold Mine Divinely Bestowed To You. God gave you what you *needed*...not what you necessarily *earned.* You are attracted to the obvious and apparent. Their greatest legacy to you is hidden, invisible and will require serious and patient pursuit.

2. You Have No Right To Anything You Have Not Pursued. That is why Jesus had the meal in the home of Zacchaeus, the evil tax collector. Zacchaeus pursued Jesus. The blind man cried out. His healing became his Harvest.

Susanne Wesley had 17 children. She invested one full day each month with each one...to determine their needs, weaknesses and Assignment. One became...the great John Wesley!

3. The Quality Of Your Questions

Reveal The Depth Of Your Caring. The Scriptures documented the long journey of the Queen of Sheba. She invested nine months of travel to meet the most famous and wealthiest king in the known world...Solomon. Her questions unlocked the profound Wisdom within him and the golden relationship for their lifetime.

    4. Keep A Dream-Journal. Observe. Listen. Assist. Document the desires, needs, fears and goals of your family. *Celebrate The Dreams... hidden deep in the imagination of your family members.* Protect their Dreams and help them grow it.

    Keeping A Dream-Journal Is Invaluable.

    Let's Pray Together...
    "Father, make me the Knowledge Bank for my family...storing Divine understanding of their needs, weaknesses, gifts and Assignments. Use me as an instrument of Wisdom in my home. In Jesus' name. Amen."

☙ 13 ❧

THE UNCOMMON FATHER KEEPS A LOVE JOURNAL.

Fathers Decide What Children Remember.
Your Memory Is A Gift Or A Curse.
You alone decide the product of your memory.

Your mind has two dominant functions: The *Imagination* and The *Memory*.

Your Imagination pre-plays a *future* event.

Your Memory re-plays a *past* event.

Painful moments will come. Waves of sadness will overwhelm every home, every family, every heart. Disappointment is inevitable.

So, The Uncommon Father must decide the joys and laughter that characterize the life you admire and desire.

1. Decide The Life Events You Want Your Children To Remember. Some are basic such as Birthdays, Anniversaries, Thanksgiving, Christmas or New Year's. Surprise moments... humorous situations...or memorable vacations require *your* planning, decision-making or *readiness.*

2. Collect Pictures Of The Events And Places You Want To Experience Together. Peruse magazines and newspapers. Question friends for their recommendations of unforgettable places or experiences.

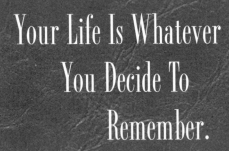

Your Life Is Whatever
You Decide To
Remember.

-MIKE MURDOCK

3.   Use Pictures To Record Memorable And Loving Moments.   Keep a throw-away camera in your glove compartment...briefcase...in the kitchen...or wherever.

4.   Seize Any Moment Worth Celebrating...And Magnify It. Others will remember wrong moments, so you must *aggressively* capture the scenes and seconds that become your Well of Memory. Your family will never forget this. Ever.

5.   Dignify, Memorialize And Memorize Your Journey Through Life By Keeping A Personal Love-Journal.

Any Life Worth Living Is Worth Documenting.

Let's Pray Together...

"Holy Spirit, You are an Author. You told us to write down our vision...document our experiences and teach our children what we want them to remember. Today, I start my Love-Journal, knowing this Seed of Obedience will birth the Harvest I long for in my family. In Jesus' name. Amen."

Decisions Decide Wealth.

-MIKE MURDOCK

⚞ **14** ⚟

THE UNCOMMON FATHER SCHEDULES MONEY-TALKS TOGETHER WITH HIS FAMILY ROUTINELY.

Your Decisions Decide Your Wealth.

Money is a *Tool*...that builds the environment, home and circumstances you dream about.

Money is a *Communicator*...that enables you to give gifts, Pictures of Remembrance. *Gifts can talk* your love when you feel incapable of choosing the appropriate words.

The Uncommon Father is always the businessman...whose decisions bring increase to his family.

1.   Embrace The Financial Philosophy And Beliefs Established By The Holy Spirit In The Word Of God. The Scriptures teach that Prosperity is the will of God...that Diligence, Integrity, Obedience, Parental Respect, Productivity, Tithing and Wisdom are the Seven Master Foundation Stones of Financial Wealth (see Psalm 112:1-3). Wisdom matters.

2.   Set Specific Money Goals With Deadlines And Details. Choose which wall in your home will become your Dream-Wall.   Keep pictures of the house, car and future you are focusing your faith toward right now. The Power is in your *Plan.*

3. Choose A Financial Mentorship Program That You Both Respect And Value. Friends or your financial advisor may recommend one for you. Select one book a month to read, underline and discuss...together.

4. Set Aside Two Hours Weekly To Review All Financial Matters Honestly And Completely. Integrity matters. Pray over your goals, plans and opportunities to solve problems for others.

Information Always Breeds Confidence.

≈ 15 ≈

THE UNCOMMON FATHER DEFINES HIS EXPECTATIONS OF HIS FAMILY CLEARLY AND CONSISTENTLY.

The Enemy Of Peace Is Confusion.

Nations, families and people fragment because of wrong words, unclear motives or undefined goals.

The Uncommon Father mentors his family on their roles, their chores and his expectations.

1. Establish A General List Of The Tasks Necessary For A Peaceful Home. This includes daily, weekly, monthly and even annual tasks. Decide clearly who is assigned to each task. Systematize the method for accountability, whether it be purchasing or paying bills.

2. Create An Environment For Mentorship And Learning. A parent once told me, "I love my child so much I even make their bed for them." I explained that she was *stealing* from her child...the golden opportunity of learning *order* and how to *give back* to a parent.

3. Recognize That Your Greatest Gift To Your Children Is An Opportunity To Become A Giver Instead Of A Taker. Taking comes easy. It seems to be human nature. Think of the newborn

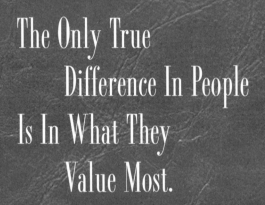

The Only True
Difference In People
Is In What They
Value Most.

-MIKE MURDOCK

baby reaching for the milk desired...without attending any seminar on it! Those who continually receive must be given The Master Gift...*the opportunity to become* a Giver.

4. Document Your Expectations And Update Them Routinely. Needs change. Focus for excellence. *Increased Information Will Always Necessitate Change.*

Unexplained Behavior Creates Bitterness. *That's why the Uncommon Father uses knowledge to prevent misunderstanding and inner pain.*

The Longevity Of Every
Relationship Is Decided
By The Willingness To Forgive.

-MIKE MURDOCK

≋ 16 ≋

THE UNCOMMON FATHER NEVER ACCEPTS REPORTS FROM OTHERS BEFORE HE HEARS THE EXPLANATION FROM HIS OWN FAMILY.

Accurate Information Matters.

Someone related that they had seen a "woman leave the hotel room" of a well-known minister. It launched a flood of accusatory statements, until someone quietly revealed...it was his sister. Incidentally, her husband had remained with the minister while she searched for the ice machine. Nobody had even considered that!

The Uncommon Father hears out a matter fully before he judges, concludes or accuses.

Mercy is his Seed.

Trust becomes his Harvest.

1. Nothing Is Ever As It First Appears. Half-truth is The Backbone of Modern Media. Yet, it has destroyed the lives and families of millions. "He that answereth a matter before he heareth it, it is folly and shame unto him" (Proverbs 18:13).

2. The First Weapon Of All Satanic Strategy Is Doubt And Unbelief. Think about the Garden of Eden. Adam and Eve were enjoying walks with God. Suddenly, the serpent injects poisonous doubt. "...Yea, hath God said, Ye shall not eat of every tree of the garden?" (Genesis 3:1). It destroyed their life and the future of the entire human race.

3.   Mark Any Satanic Relationship That Increases Your Confusion Instead Of Your Peace. Paul said, "Be not deceived: evil communications corrupt good manners" (1 Corinthians 15:33). *Remember This.*

Missing Information Makes Conclusions Impossible.

The Uncommon Father makes listening his Tool. It provides an avalanche of accurate information...and a lifetime of loyalty from his family.

≈ 17 ≈

THE UNCOMMON FATHER PRAYS FOR SPECIFIC METHODS TO MEET THE NEEDS OF HIS FAMILY.

The Holy Spirit Is Your Mentor.

He knows your family better than you. He has knowledge of the childhood pain, disappointments and fears. He knows the deepest yearnings of their heart. The Holy Spirit knows your family more than they know themselves.

Listen to Him. Reach for His knowledge.

1. The Holy Spirit Loves Your Family Even More Than You Ever Will. Remember this! The Spirit decided your Assignment...to them. So, He will advise, counsel and continuously mentor you on how to minister, protect and strengthen them. "I will instruct thee and teach thee in the way which thou shalt go: I will guide thee with Mine eye" (Psalm 32:8).

2. Any Sincere Prayer For Divine Wisdom Is Guaranteed An Answer From God. "If any of you lack wisdom, let him ask of God, that giveth to all men liberally, and upbraideth not; and it shall be given him" (James 1:5). The more specific your prayer request, the greater your faith.

3. What God Has Stored In You For Your Family Is Your Point Of Difference From All

Your Success Is
Decided By
Your Difference
From Others.

-MIKE MURDOCK

Others. Expect The Holy Spirit to reveal hidden opportunities to minister *strategically.*

Father, you are not carrying your load alone. The Holy Spirit is continuously advising you, empowering you and listening every moment for your whispers for help.

Expect Supernatural impartation from the Holy Spirit...in every crisis moment.

God Never, Never, Never Fails.

When Fatigue
Walks In
Faith Walks Out.

-MIKE MURDOCK

❧ 18 ❧

THE UNCOMMON FATHER PLAYS AS HARD AS HE WORKS.

Rest Is As Important As Work.

Work is mentioned in the Bible 420 times. *Rest* is mentioned 275 times. Both are essential.

The Uncommon Father knows the remarkable restoration rest produces. Laughter time replenishes, renews, restores.

1. The Season Of Rest And Renewal Is Sacred, Holy And Commanded. After creating the universe, the animals and the human race, God rested. "And God blessed the seventh day, and sanctified it: because that in it He had rested from all His work" (Genesis 2:3; see also Matthew 11:28,29).

2. Jesus Scheduled Seasons Of Rest, Change And Renewal For His Own Disciples. "And He said unto them, Come ye yourselves apart into a desert place, and rest a while: for there were many coming and going, and they had no leisure so much as to eat" (Mark 6:31).

3. Every Vacation Should Have A Chosen Theme. One leader chooses a different focus each year...golf, learning Spanish or deep-sea diving. "To every thing there is a season, and a time to every purpose under the heaven" (Ecclesiastes 3:1).

4.   The Rhythm And Regularity Of Your Stress-Free Fun Season Will Actually Increase Your Productivity. "A time to weep, and a time to laugh; a time to mourn, and a time to dance" (Ecclesiastes 3:4). One pastor said, "My Friday Focus is my family exclusively.   It has revolutionized our love for each other and the ministry as well. I enjoy my church now more than ever."

Any great habit can be learned.

The Uncommon Father practices the Art of Restoration through vacation schedules, fun days and celebrations.

RECOMMENDED FOR YOUR WISDOM LIBRARY:
B-171   Seeds Of Wisdom On Motivating Yourself (32 pages/$5)
TS-41   The School Of Wisdom, Volume 1: The Uncommon
        Life (6 tapes/$30)
Order Today! www.TheWisdomCenter.tv

Silence Can Never Be Misquoted.

-MIKE MURDOCK

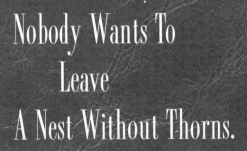

Nobody Wants To
Leave
A Nest Without Thorns.

-MIKE MURDOCK

❧ 19 ❧

THE UNCOMMON FATHER NEVER BETRAYS A SHARED CONFIDENCE FROM HIS FAMILY WITH OTHERS.

――――▷⦿◁――――

Trust Is A Treasured Gift.

Fathers hear everything. Every disappointment, every offense, every fear, every doubt. The Uncommon Father is the Harbor of Confidentiality. He refuses to reveal information that damages those he loves. He is trustworthy.

1. Every Human Heart Contains Secrets. Every family has habits, weaknesses, fantasies, childhood memories...hidden deep inside. Unspoken needs and longings lie deep inside us. The yearning of the human heart for someone to trust is profound and unchanging.

2. God Designed The Family To Be A Safe Haven In A Dangerous World. When God links you with the family of His choice, you should not have to live guarded, afraid and constantly in fear.

3. Those Who Want To Be Feared... Should Be Feared. They are deadly. Those who rule through threat instead of mentorship are satanic tools that destroy hope, faith and confidence.

4.   The Trustworthy Father Is Never Dangerous.   Their conduct is decided by their character, not opportunity.   The Uncommon Wife is likewise described, "The heart of her husband doth safely trust in her," (Proverbs 31:11).

Your family is human.   Failure is inevitable. Give them what you yourself long for...the *safety of discretion.*

It is so easy to serve someone who can be trusted.

5.   The Proof Of Loyalty Is Discretion. Father, can you be trusted with the hidden secrets confided to you by your family?

The Home Without Fear Is Heaven On Earth.

You, The Uncommon Father, can make it so.

RECOMMENDED FOR YOUR WISDOM LIBRARY:
B-136   The Wisdom Commentary, Volume 1 (256 pages/$100)
Order Today! www.TheWisdomCenter.tv

The Proof Of Love
Is
The Obsession To Protect.

-*MIKE MURDOCK*

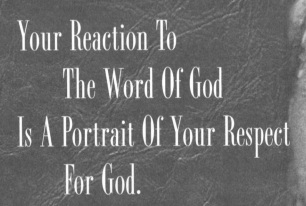

Your Reaction To
    The Word Of God
Is A Portrait Of Your Respect
    For God.

-MIKE MURDOCK

≈ 20 ≈

THE UNCOMMON FATHER MAKES THE WORD OF GOD THE STANDARD FOR HIS PERSONAL CONDUCT.

The Bible Is The Master Standard For Character.
The Word of God contains the Secrets for Successful Relationships...especially the happy family. The Uncommon Father knows that The Word of God contains the Secrets of Life in raising his family and sculpting a Godly home.

1. The Word Of God Establishes The Responsibility And Protocol Of The Children. "Children, obey your parents in the Lord: for this is right. Honour thy father and mother; (which is the first commandment with promise;) That it may be well with thee, and thou mayest live long on the earth" (Ephesians 6:1-3).

2. The Word Of God Establishes The Responsibility Of The Parents. "And, ye fathers, provoke not your children to wrath: but bring them up in the nurture and admonition of the Lord" (Ephesians 6:4). "For no man ever yet hated his own flesh; but nourisheth and cherisheth it, even as the Lord the church:" (Ephesians 5:29).

3. The Word Of God Teaches The Desired Environment And Protocol Of The

Happy Family. "Wherefore take unto you the whole armour of God, that ye may be able to withstand in the evil day, and having done all, to stand. Stand therefore, having your loins girt about with truth, and having on the breastplate of righteousness; And your feet shod with the preparation of the gospel of peace; Above all, taking the shield of faith, wherewith ye shall be able to quench all the fiery darts of the wicked. And take the helmet of salvation, and the sword of the Spirit, which is the word of God: Praying always with all prayer and supplication in the Spirit," (Ephesians 6:13-18).

4.   **The Dominant Quality Of The Spirit Is Kindness...In Every Situation.**

A.   Kindness is *commanded.* "...kind one to another" (Ephesians 4:32).

B.   The Proof of Love is *kindness.* "...[love] is kind;" (1 Corinthians 13:4).

C.   Kindness is *a God-Quality.* "God:...is of great kindness," (Joel 2:13).

D.   Kindness is a work of The Holy Spirit. "...kindness, by the Holy Ghost" (2 Corinthians 6:6).

Let's Pray Together...
"Father, the home was intended to be a haven of protection, education and significance. I ask You today for the Divine Wisdom necessary to start the journey to wholeness, peace and a stress-free environment. Make me the Instrument of Change in Your hand. My faith is in Your power, Your promises and unchanging commitment to my home. In Jesus' name. Amen."

≈ 21 ≈

THE UNCOMMON FATHER STRIVES TO CREATE A STRESS-FREE ENVIRONMENT FOR HIS FAMILY.

Daily Life Is Usually Daily Warfare.
You experience this every morning. Motivating your family toward order...bumper-to-bumper traffic every morning en route to work...emotional confrontations with unhappy and critical co-workers...expectations from others that fragment your focus. Life is battle. Continuous, unending and sometimes almost unbearable.

Every Human Longs For A Nest Without Thorns. An unspoken thirst for a non-critical climate. An Oasis on the Desert of Life. An Environment of Escape from shattering disappointments.

The Uncommon Father seeks to make his home a...Nest Without Thorns for his family. He too, knows the suffocation of people-expectations. He feels the torrent of tasks flooding his daily schedule. He can feel the unspoken frustrations. He senses and anticipates the unmet needs of those he loves. He just knows. He cares. He responds.

That is why he is Uncommon.

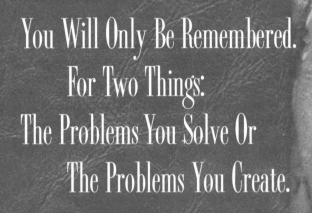

You Will Only Be Remembered.
For Two Things:
The Problems You Solve Or
   The Problems You Create.

-MIKE MURDOCK

The Uncommon Father is a Rose in a World of Thorns. He births the Fragrance so desperately needed...when the stench of disrespect is choking out the life around those he loves. He WILLINGLY reaches to help heal and pour the healing words of care.

When others are sneering, his *countenance* exudes caring.

When others are demanding, he demonstrates *Servanthood*.

When others withdraw, he *reaches*...to pour *healing* words.

8 Keys In Creating A Stress-Free Environment For Someone You Love

1. Reflect On Their Responsibilities, Spoken And Unknown. Every member of your family carries an invisible burden others can never discern. Fears, painful memories, unfulfilled expectations and the collection of disappointments continually occurring.

2. Ask Questions Of True Interest About Their Chosen And Dominant Focus. You can only do this after you have learned the magnetism of listening. It was the Secret of Abigail, who knew what David needed to hear when his anger exploded like an uncontrollable raging fire.

3. Assess Any Environment Before You Attempt To Enter It, Alter Or Influence It. It is common to observe a small child who enters a funeral home giggling or playful, simply because they are too inexperienced to evaluate the environment. The Wise are different. *The Uncommon Father observes, identifies and respects the immediate focus of others.* He patiently waits for the right timing before initiating any changes in conversation or focus. As one wife explained to me, "Monday night is my husband's night of relaxation. He enjoys sports, and that is the night for me to respect his need to watch his favorite game, football. It is disrespectful for me to ignore that distinctive passion and need in him."

4. Create The Atmosphere-Routine Unique And Distinctive To Those You Love. What are their Top 10 Favorite Songs? Create 3 CDs of those songs. (One for their home, their car and a back-up kept in their closet safe.)

What is their favorite room fragrance? Use candles, sprays, potpourri or whatever is necessary...and saturate the house with it before they enter.

What are their favorite munchies? Have handy and waiting for them, the plate of carrots, celery sticks and radishes they like.

What are their favorite magazines? Position them next to their favorite place to sit and relax.

5. Present Your Concerns Requesting Their Participation Instead Of The Tone Of Accusation. One minister friend of mine always approaches me gingerly, carefully with profound graciousness. He does not say, "I disagree with you." He begins, "That is an interesting viewpoint. What are your thoughts about the other side others might take...?" Then, he presents what I have already discerned is his own chosen position and view. His graciousness is magnetic. He is statesman-like in presenting another opinion. It is not an attempt to be clever, deceptive or manipulating. He has learned to activate participation instead of defensiveness.

6. Listen Continuously To The Inner Voice Of The Holy Spirit. He will mentor you internally, intuitively in how to pleasure those you love. A profound statement from one of my closest friends radically changed me. He was teaching his church and said, "You ask me if I am a people-pleaser. I sincerely want to be. I will do everything possible to be pleasing to others. I want others to be pleasured by my presence. That is the desire of God for us to bless and be pleasing to each other." I sat there stunned, as the dawning of this truth broke across my heart. We have distorted the scripture about pleasing God, rather than man. He was teaching us the *priority* of obedience to God...*not* to disrespect those around us.

7. Embrace Unreservedly The Privilege And Assignment Of Serving Those God Has Given You To Love. Empty yourself as a purposeful Seed into others. God guarantees the reward, the increase and the inevitable Favor. *What You Make Happen For Others, God Will Make Happen For You.* "Knowing that whatsoever good thing any man doeth, the same shall he receive of the Lord, whether he be bond or free" (Ephesians 6:8).

You are creating a memory today.
For yourself.
For others.

8.   Decide To Become An Instrument Of Pleasure, Not Pain. The Word is always your Wisdom. "We then that are strong ought to bear the infirmities of the weak, and not to please ourselves. Let every one of us please his neighbour for his good to edification. For even Christ pleased not Himself; but, as it is written, The reproaches of them that reproached thee fell on me" (Romans 15:1-3).

❧ 22 ❧

THE UNCOMMON FATHER RECOGNIZES, TREASURES AND EMBRACES WISE COUNSEL WHEREVER HE FINDS IT.

━━━▷◦◁━━━

Wisdom Often Arrives Camouflaged.

It is hidden in surprising packages...so only the passionate qualify to receive it.

The best gifts in life rarely come in silk and satin. God often hides His greatest gifts in plain and common wrappings. Jesus arrived as a baby in a manger. His riding into Jerusalem on a small donkey did not reflect the image of a true King of Kings to the religious minds of His day.

Picture a tired, weary old traveller. He is aging, and his camels are thirsty and exhausted. Yet, he represented the entire wealth of Abraham...as Rebekkah discovered within hours.

Naaman, a Syrian general, has leprosy. He eats meals with kings. He has hundreds of men under his leadership. He is wealthy, well-known and a proven genius among men. But, *his housekeeper knows something he does not know.* She knows about the mantle of miracles on the prophet, Elisha.

Note the Scriptural account. "Now Naaman,

The Willingness To Listen
Is The First Step
Toward An Uncommon Life.

-MIKE MURDOCK

captain of the host of the king of Syria, was a great man with his master, and honourable, because by him the Lord had given deliverance unto Syria: he was also a mighty man in valour, but he was a leper. And the Syrians had gone out by companies, and had brought away captive out of the land of Israel a little maid; and she waited on Naaman's wife. And she said unto her mistress, Would God my lord were with the prophet that is in Samaria! for he would recover him of his leprosy" (read 2 Kings 5:1-3).

Naaman accepted the advice of *someone of lower rank*...and received his healing from leprosy.

Treasuring Wise Counsel Is The Master Secret To All Success. The Uncommon Father knows this.

9 Facts To Remember In Hearing The Voice Of God

1. God Wants To Talk To You About His Plans For You. "For I know the thoughts that I think toward you, saith the Lord, thoughts of peace, and not of evil, to give you an expected end" (Jeremiah 29:11).

2. God Planted His Greatness Within You To Accomplish Great Exploits For The Kingdom. "...but the people that do know their God shall be strong, and do exploits" (Daniel 11:32).

3. God Wants You To Do Something Nobody Else Has Been Able To Do. "Verily, verily, I say unto you, He that believeth on Me, the works that I do shall he do also; and greater works than these shall he do; because I go unto My Father" (John 14:12).

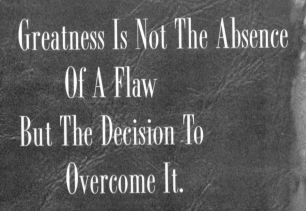

Greatness Is Not The Absence
Of A Flaw
But The Decision To
Overcome It.

-MIKE MURDOCK

4.   God Will Instruct You Toward Your Future, Away From Your Past. "Remember ye not the former things, neither consider the things of old. Behold, I will do a new thing; now it shall spring forth; shall ye not know it? I will even make a way in the wilderness, and rivers in the desert" (Isaiah 43:18,19).

5.   God Wants You To Enter Into Solitude With Him, Away From Distracting Voices Of Wrong Counsel. "Be still, and know that I am God: I will be exalted among the heathen, I will be exalted in the earth" (Psalm 46:10). Every great relationship is exposed to others' voices, "the third party." God enjoyed Adam and Eve. Then, satan entered as "the third party" and destroyed the beautiful scenario of love and agreement. The Holy Spirit clothed Samson with supernatural strength. Then, Delilah entered as "the third party." Every day of your life, a third voice threatens to stain what God is trying to do for your life. Identify it, expose it and confront it...ruthlessly.

6.   God Uses Even Children To Speak Into Our Lives. "...and a little child shall lead them" (Isaiah 11:6).

7.   God Even Uses Small Insects To Mentor Us! "Go to the ant, thou sluggard; consider her ways, and be wise: Which having no guide, overseer, or ruler, Provideth her meat in the summer, and gathereth her food in the harvest" (Proverbs 6:6-8).

8.   God Uses Seasons And Times Of Opportunity To Reveal Guidance And Direction To Us. "To every thing there is a season, and a time to every purpose under the heaven:" (Ecclesiastes 3:1).

9. God Wants To Reveal The Secrets Of Life To Us. "He revealeth the deep and secret things: He knoweth what is in the darkness, and the light dwelleth with Him" (Daniel 2:22).

The Uncommon Father knows that God can even use a talking donkey to arrest the attention of a prophet...a large fish to swallow a rebellious prophet...and a small raven to feed a man of God during a famine.

Look for God...in everything. EVERYTHING. His Hand is there. His Voice is there. His Wisdom is there.

The Uncommon Life Becomes Uncommon When You Can Recognize Divine Counsel...Regardless Of The Packaging Or Method God Uses.

❧ 23 ❧

THE UNCOMMON FATHER CAN BE TRUSTED BY THOSE HE LOVES.

━━━━▶▷◉◁◀━━━━

The Story Of Abigail Fascinates Me.

She was married to Nabal, a wealthy fool. His genius with multiplying money was obvious. His recognition of greatness was faulty and revealed his character.

What You Recognize Often Reveals What You Are. Remember Jesus died between two thieves. One cursed Him, but one recognized Him as the Son of God. The Pharisees did not discern that Jesus was truly the Christ. But Zacchaeus, the unwholesome tax collector did recognize Him as the Christ. Jesus went home with him to sow more counsel and ministry.

▶ *What You Discern Reveals What You Desire.*

▶ *What You Discern Reveals What You Are.*

▶ *Your Discernment Reveals Your Character.*

Here is another scenario. David's army is starved. He sends 10 men as his ambassadors and representatives to Nabal, a wealthy landowner. The request is for food. Nabal curses them and sneers that David is a nobody, unimportant and a fool.

David explodes. He is angry. His warrior heart required revenge and retaliation. David makes a

The Unwillingness To Trust
The Right Person
Will Create More Losses
Than The Mistake Of
Trusting The Wrong Person.

-MIKE MURDOCK

public vow to destroy everything and anyone linked to Nabal. Meanwhile...the servants of Nabal and his wife, Abigail, are distraught. The skills of David are known. So is his obsession for rightness.

The servants inform Abigail privately of Nabal's insult to David's men. They risked embarrassment, being misunderstood and even being killed by breaking the Code of Silence regarding the decision-making of their boss and leader, Nabal.

But, they trusted Abigail. The Uncommon Woman! They trusted her discretion, her decision-making and judgment. The servants discerned her *difference* from Nabal, her husband. She was approachable, truthful, sensitive and wise.

The Uncommon Father...is also approachable, sensitive and fair.

5 Facts About Trusting Others

1. There Is A Difference In Trusting Someone's Character And Someone's Expertise. A lawyer may have a greed problem but be brilliant in presenting his court cases. You trust his expertise and giftings, but not his integrity. He may win your case, but you are forced to analyze every bill carefully for overcharge.

2. Trusting Someone Is Different Than Loving Someone. God loved the world. He loves us as His family. But, God knows we are humans, with flaws, wrong judgments and more mistakes.

3. Time Will Reveal What Interrogation Cannot. You can ask a thousand questions and still be deceived by others. But, when you observe the continual fruit from someone's life over Time, information emerges that you would never have known.

4.   Someone You Are Trusting Is Usually Trusting Someone Else You Would Not. Sit in The Samson Seminar. He trusted Delilah and she trusted the evil leaders who she worked with. Samson did not tell his secret to them. He trusted Delilah...she processed the information to others wanting to kill him.

5.   Distrusting The Right Person Will Create More Losses In Your Life Than Trusting The Wrong Person. Everyone knows the sorrow, losses and pain of trusting a wrong, deceptive person with our inner secrets. The pain is indescribable. The losses devastate us emotionally. But, refusing to trust the *right* people is even *more* deadly and devastating. When good people advise you wisely, embrace and respect the counsel enough to follow it. That is one of the qualities in Abigail that is remarkable. Her husband was rich, his servants were poor. But, she knew who to believe.

That is one of the Most Important Keys To Success...Decide Who To Believe! It reveals what you already are within you.

The Uncommon Father Knows Who To Believe.

6 Areas You Should Be Trustworthy

1.   You Should Be Trustworthy Of Protecting The Reputation Of Good People Not Present. True loyalty will not allow others to speak evil of those you love...without them present. "A talebearer revealeth secrets: but he that is of a faithful spirit concealeth the matter" (Proverbs 11:13).

2. **You Should Be Trustworthy To Be Diligent Every Moment You Are Receiving A Salary For Working.** "Redeeming the time, because the days are evil" (Ephesians 5:16). I phoned a pastor friend one day. He was out of town. When I apologized for interrupting his secretary's work, she replied, "Oh, I have all the time in the world. He's not at work, so we are having a blast here!" My heart sank...when I realized my friend had hired untrustworthy people around him. I made him aware of their character upon his return.

3. **You Should Be Trustworthy In Accuracy And Integrity Of Your Words And Views.** Truthfulness confirms your right standing with God. "He that speaketh truth sheweth forth righteousness: but a false witness deceit" (Proverbs 12:17). It is sad to watch someone nod in agreement with someone in conversation and then take the opposite side after leaving their presence. Say what you really believe. Always believe what you have chosen to say.

4. **You Should Be Trustworthy In Doing What You Say You Will Do.** "But let your communication be, Yea, yea; Nay, nay: for whatsoever is more than these cometh of evil" (Matthew 5:37). If you promise to meet someone at 10:00 a.m., do not show up at 11:00 a.m. *Do what you promise.* If you have made a faith promise to a ministry for $1,000, do not use it to buy a new color television and then claim, "God never gave me the money to pay my vow."

5. You Should Be Trustworthy To Finish What You Begin. It is what made the Apostle Paul an Uncommon Man of God. "I have fought a good fight, I have finished my course, I have kept the faith:" (2 Timothy 4:7). The Spirit of a Finisher is irreplaceable. One boss once said, "I have fifty full-time employees but only two will finish what I give them to do. I only have two who do not require my coaxing, motivation and follow-up." "Seest thou a man diligent in his business? he shall stand before kings; he shall not stand before mean men" (Proverbs 22:29).

6. You Should Be Trustworthy In Paying Your Bills. I have seen people become angry when their credit card payment came due. Yet, they are the ones who created the bill! Others become incensed toward a bank for repossessing a car...but, they refused to keep their promise to pay! I know of one desperate husband whose wife refuses to move to a less expensive home...and *both* are destroying their very family through *overwork*.

Do not buy what you cannot pay for.

Develop trustworthiness. Are you facing a huge indebtedness resulting from an illness or financial setback? Then, pay the bill off $10 each week. But, show your integrity by taking small steps toward the complete payoff...weekly.

Sometimes, you will meet people who refuse to trust you even when you are trustworthy. They have had painful experiences, troubling memories and bitter disappointments in their past. They have taken the position that you, too, should not be trusted. Day after day, week after week, you may discover that all your faithfulness and consistency is ignored. They simply refuse to believe in you, trust you or acknowledge your record of faithfulness. Withdraw from their life. *Do not expose yourself to continual emotional assault and mind abuse.* "Let not then your good be evil spoken of:" (Romans 14:16). Even God Himself requires trust before He builds a relationship with you.

For several years, I tried very, very hard to build a friendship with someone I loved. Quite deeply. Nothing I did was ever enough. When I finally pointed out all the gifts I had provided for them, including a house and car. The reaction stunned me.

"But, you give to everyone, not just me. So, why would your gifts prove your love?"

I was speechless. I realized this person did not want the *responsibility* for believing in my love. *To accept my love would require adaptation, change and corresponding conduct that celebrated it.*

Let's Pray Together...

"Holy Spirit, develop within me a heart of purity, integrity and complete trustworthiness. Kill anything in me that stops others from experiencing YOU Who lives within me. Forgive me of every inconsistency. Unlock a new passion for truth. I will be trustworthy in every friendship in my life. In Jesus' name. Amen."

The Proof Of Legitimate Authority
Is The Passion To
Provide, Protect And Promote.

-MIKE MURDOCK

24

THE UNCOMMON FATHER SUBMITS TO THOSE GOD HAS PLACED IN DIVINE AUTHORITY OVER HIS LIFE.

The Uncommon Father Honors Authority.

18 Facts About Authority And Divine Order

1. **Order Is The Accurate Arrangement Of Things.** Think for a moment. What if your nose were on top of your head? You would drown the very first rain, wouldn't you? What if your eyes were on the bottom of your feet? What a task it would become to simply walk! It is almost laughable, isn't it? Every thing created has a Divine function, purpose, reason.

Imagine your legs complaining to your arms. "You just hang there all day long. I have to carry you everywhere!" Your legs instinctively discern their function, their purpose and their product.

2. **Authority, Instructions And Order Are Three Important Forces In Your Life.** The purpose of Authority is to create, impart and enforce the instructions that birth and keep Order.

What is the purpose of traffic lights, stop signs

and every highway sign? To keep every car in its place, its path. Would you want a highway without ANY instructions, without ANY warnings or information? Can you imagine the nightmare of car pile-ups, accidents, broken and torn bodies across a freeway...if no warning signs existed?

3. Disorder Guarantees Tragedies, Losses And Pain. Every mechanical failure on an airplane verifies this.

4. The Rewards Of Order Are Peace, Productivity, Profit And Comfort. When the clothes in your closet are "in order" you actually feel good and happy about your life. Why? *Order.*

5. Any Movement Towards Order Generates Pleasure. Who should decide and impart these highway instructions? Just anyone? Of course not. The teenage driver would say, "Don't try to limit me in my speed. My car was created to go 140 mph. Don't give me instructions." Then, the funeral homes would be full and our nation would become chaotic very swiftly. Drinkers would approve of driving while drunk...and the bodies of babies would be splattered across the highways.

6. The Responsibility Of Authority Is Decision-Making. I overheard an agitated customer complaining to a discount store clerk. The clerk wearily insisted, "Ma'am, I am sorry but I cannot help you. My manager is the only one who can make that decision." The manager was the Authority, the Decision-Maker in that scenario and situation.

7. An Authority Is The Person Who Is Qualified Or Assigned The Responsibility Of

Making A Decision Involving Others. That is why we vote for Senators, Representatives, Governors, Mayors and even Presidents. We "authorize" them through our public voting to BECOME THE AUTHORITY AND DECISION-MAKER of the rules that govern our city, our roads, our education, our prisons. In return, our armed forces stand guard for us...school teachers show up to teach our children in school...criminals are caught by police...and judges send them to prison.

8. **Authority Makes Rules And Give Instructions To Establish Order In An Environment.** This is the function of police, mayors, governors and civic leaders.

9. **The Proof Of Legitimate Authority Is Peace, Protection And Provision.** When God establishes an Authority over your life, you should experience Divine peace, Divine protection and Divine financial provision.

Jesus is the Authority over the Church, the body of Christ. "For the husband is the head of the wife, even as Christ is the head of the church: and He is the saviour of the body. Therefore as the church is subject unto Christ, so let the wives be to their own husbands in every thing. Husbands, love your wives, even as Christ also loved the church, and gave Himself for it;" (Ephesians 5:23-25).

10. **Divine Order In The Home Is That The Father Is The Authority To Protect His Family.** This becomes his responsibility to love them, protect them, provide for them. Remember, the proof of genuine spiritual authority includes provision.

Submission Only Begins
When
Agreement Ends.

-MIKE MURDOCK

11. The Parents Are Established By God As The Divine Authority Over Their Children. They are Scripturally commanded and expected to protect, provide and promote the excellence and success of their children. How? Instructions. Discipline. "Only take heed to thyself, and keep thy soul diligently, lest thou forget the things which thine eyes have seen, and lest they depart from thy heart all the days of thy life: but teach them thy sons, and thy sons' sons;" (Deuteronomy 4:9).

12. The Scriptures Establish Authority To Give Instructions That Create Order. The proof of Order is peace, prosperity, productivity and protection (see John 10:10; 3 John 1:2).

13. When A Child Honors The Authority Of Their Parents, God Promises Promotions And Blessing To That Child. *Order guarantees rewards.* "Honour thy father and thy mother, as the Lord thy God hath commanded thee; that thy days may be prolonged, and that it may go well with thee, in the land which the Lord thy God giveth thee" (Deuteronomy 5:16).

14. Right Instructions Increase Order, Productivity And Profits. "My son, if thou wilt receive my words, and hide my commandments with thee; Then shalt thou understand the fear of the Lord, and find the knowledge of God" (Proverbs 2:1,5).

15. The Embracing Of Divine Authority Reveals The Fear Of God, The Beginning Of Supernatural Wisdom. "The fear of the Lord is the beginning of wisdom: and the knowledge of the holy is understanding" (Proverbs 9:10).

16. The Fear Of God Guarantees The Divine Favor And Provision Of God. "By humility and the fear of the Lord are riches, and honour, and life" (Proverbs 22:4).

17. The Fear Of God Qualifies You For An Uncommon Relationship With The Holy Spirit And His Level Of Success For You. "Blessed is the man that feareth the Lord, that delighteth greatly in His commandments. His seed shall be mighty upon earth: the generation of the upright shall be blessed. Wealth and riches shall be in his house: and his righteousness endureth for ever" (Psalm 112:1-3).

18. The Obedience To Correct Instructions From Divine Authority Guarantee A Longer Life. "My son, forget not My law; but let thine heart keep My commandments: For length of days, and long life, and peace, shall they add to thee" (Proverbs 3:1,2).

5 Steps Toward Divine Protection

1. Recognize The Divine Function Of Authority Over Your Life. If you have been abused by it, forgive and believe God will turn it for your own.

2. Receive Divine Strength And Impartation To Submit To Those In Authority Over You. You cannot do this alone. You will never have the strength of the spirit to submit to another.

3. Remember That Your Reaction To Authority Is Your Response To God. When you submit to Divine Design, God moves in waves of

Favor toward you.

4. Remind Yourself That Submission Does Not Truly Begin Until Agreement Ends. It hurts. It can make you feel stripped of your significance and importance. It will force any hidden rebellion in you to emerge. *Correction Upward Is Always Rebellion.* "For rebellion is as the sin of witchcraft, and stubbornness is as iniquity and idolatry. Because thou hast rejected the word of the Lord, He hath also rejected thee from being king" (1 Samuel 15:23).

5. Remember That Rewarding Those Under Your Own Authority Is A Scriptural Command And Follow It. "Withhold not good from them to whom it is due, when it is in the power of thine hand to do it" (Proverbs 3:27).

Father, I urge you to invest in 12 teaching sessions I did at The Wisdom Center. Six cassettes and nothing else like them (only $30)...called "The Law Of Order."

Order begins with your attitude. Today!

Anger Is The Birthplace For Change.

-MIKE MURDOCK

❧ 25 ❧

THE UNCOMMON FATHER TURNS EVERY ANGER MOMENT INTO A PRAYER PROJECT.

———◆———

Anger Is Disappointment.

Anger is desperation-disappointment that craves expression. Anger is an attempt to alter that disappointment and turn it around through force, threat or control.

The Uncommon Father harnesses that anger and turns it into a Prayer Project. I learned that from my own father, my mentor.

My mother was 13 years old when she met my father, 16 years old. They married when she became 14. Her father had died, and the teenage girl launched into an entire new world of change. Seven children later, she shared some profound mentorship into me. Her deep painful disappointment with disobedient children often burst out in the form of anger. During an emotional outburst of her great exasperation one afternoon, I asked, "Mother, do you ever wish you had not had us children?"

She sighed with a half-smile, "Many times."

"Did you ever want to run away from home and

get away from all of us?" I half-joked.

She responded with a slight grimace, "Many times, but, I didn't have anywhere to go."

My mother experienced continual disapproval, confrontation, disagreement and painful verbal assaults from church members, in-laws and older brothers. Only eternity will reveal the remarkable comebacks she made from these heartbreaking experiences.

But, there was a daily experience in our home that happened without fail. It happened every single day for the 18 years I was home. We had two family altars a day, every morning and every night. Mother would pore over scripture after scripture, in persistent *search for a promise from God to claim, believe and hold on to.* She would find that Divine promise and memorize it, quote it, teach and pray it...continuously.

Anger drove her to the Word of God and prayer.

Anger birthed her pursuit...of *answers*, of God, of The Secret of Peace.

7 Facts About Anger And Change

1. **Pain And Disappointment In Life Is Inevitable.** God is God...and yet He, too, experiences pain and disappointment from human rejection and disobedience every single day. Jesus poured out His love, His life, His healing power and still experienced hatred, scorn and sarcasm from the religious leaders of His day. *He was perfect...yet experienced anger.*

His difference was how He *focused* His

anger...to *create change*.

2.   Anger Is A Clue To Your Anointing And Assignment. When Moses saw an Egyptian beating an Israelite, anger rose up within him. That anger was a clue. It was a signal. The situation that infuriated him was the one God had ordained him to change, correct and alter. Yes, *anger reveals the anointing on your life*. "And it shall come to pass in that day, that his burden shall be taken away from off thy shoulder, and his yoke from off thy neck, and the yoke shall be destroyed because of the anointing" (Isaiah 10:27).

3.   Anger Is The Birthplace Of Change. Situations only change when anger is born. You will not solve a problem, consciously or unconsciously, until you experience a holy and righteous anger rising up within you.

4.   You Will Not Change A Situation Until It Becomes Unbearable. For many years in the South, African-Americans experienced tragic injustice. It might still be occurring today had it not been for a courageous woman named Rosa Parks. This work-weary black lady took her place in the back of a crowded bus in Montgomery, Alabama. When the bus filled, she refused to stand for a white man to have her seat. It was the catalyst for dramatic, appropriate and long-needed change in America. That kind of courage deserves honor and respect...and continuation.

5.   Whatever You Can Tolerate, You Cannot Change. Whatever you refuse to accept, whatever makes you mad enough to take action, is a clue to your Assignment.

MADD, Mothers Against Drunk Driving, was started by a mother who saw her child killed on the street by a drunken driver. Her anger birthed a majestic and admirable reaction.

6. You Must Become Angry About The Present Before The Future Will Listen To You.

7. If You Can Adapt To Your Present, You Will Never Enter Your Future. Only those who cannot tolerate the present are qualified to enter their future.

It has happened in my own life. When I was a teenager, I felt a great attraction to the courtroom. I wanted to be an attorney. I sat for hours in those courtrooms in my little hometown of Lake Charles, Louisiana. I took notes by the hour on cases that came up. I still have a hatred of injustice.

I can become angry about it right now while I am writing you this chapter, just thinking about people who have not been represented properly. I read law books continually and still continually read books dealing with the legal system. Watching the process of law and observing the manipulation that occurs in the courtroom still infuriates me. I believe this *anger is a clue to the anointing on my life.*

Ignorance angers me. When I talk to people who are uninformed, something comes alive in me. A desire to teach is overwhelming. I speak at seminars throughout the world. Sometimes I almost miss my airplane schedule because I become so obsessed with teaching that to walk out of the seminar becomes extremely difficult.

Unproductive employees are a source of great

agitation to me. I believe it is a clue to a mantle on my life. It is important to me that I unlock the mystery of achievement through Wisdom Keys and books that I write.

Listen carefully to ministers who teach about prosperity. *They hate poverty.* They despise lack. It grieves them deeply to see families wounded, destroyed and devastated because of poverty. Their messages are full of fury and sound almost angry! Why? Destroying poverty is a calling *within* them.

Have you ever listened to ministers who have an anointing for deliverance? They become angry toward demonic spirits that possess family members.

Listen to a soul-winning evangelist. Do you hear his passion? He is moved with compassion when he sees the unsaved and those who are uncommitted to Christ.

The Uncommon Father seizes moments of anger as waves toward intercession, change and movement.

Anger Is The Birthplace For Miracles.

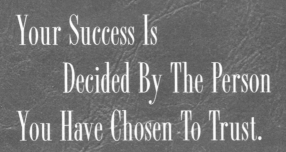

Your Success Is
    Decided By The Person
You Have Chosen To Trust.

-MIKE MURDOCK

❧ 26 ❧

THE UNCOMMON FATHER EXPECTS MIRACLES AND DIVINE ASSISTANCE FROM THE HOLY SPIRIT.

No Father Can Succeed Alone.

God designed His own necessity in your life. The Uncommon Father accepts this fact.

9 Facts Every Father Should Remember About His Assignment

1. Every Assignment Will Require Supernatural Intervention Of God. Jesus said it: "...for without Me ye can do nothing" (John 15:5). Your Assignment will require miracles.

Miracles require God.

God requires your obedience.

When Joshua and the Israelites approached Jericho, it took a miracle to bring the walls down.

When Gideon and his 300 men took on the huge army of the Midianites, victory required an absolute miracle.

When Naaman dipped in the Jordan River to receive healing of his leprosy, it took a miracle for the healing to occur.

When the wine ran out at the marriage in

Cana, it took a miracle of Jesus for the water in the water pots to be turned into wine.

When the widow of Zarephath was eating her last meal, it required a miracle for it to multiply. The Harvest from her Seed fed her, Elijah and her son for the rest of the famine season.

When the armies of Pharaoh chased the Israelites, their drowning in the Red Sea required a miracle.

2. God Never Gives You An Assignment That Does Not Require His Participation. He keeps Himself necessary in His world!

3. Your Assignment Will Always Be Big Enough To Require A Miracle. You will *not* be able to do your Assignment *alone*. You cannot complete your Assignment without the continuous, obvious and necessary *hand of God*.

You are wanting a *miracle*.

God is wanting a *relationship*.

He makes miracles *necessary* so that you will be motivated to *pursue Him* and His involvement in your life.

4. God Will Never Involve Himself In A Dream That You Can Achieve Alone.

5. Every Single Act Of God Is Designed To Increase Your Dependency Upon Him And Your Addiction To Him And His Presence. "And He humbled thee, and suffered thee to hunger, and fed thee with manna, which thou knewest not, neither did thy fathers know; that He might make thee know that man doth not live by bread only, but by every word that proceedeth out of the mouth of the Lord doth man live" (Deuteronomy 8:3).

6. Your Heavenly Father Refuses To Be Forgotten And Ignored. "Beware that thou forget not the Lord thy God, in not keeping His commandments, and His judgments, and His statutes, which I command thee this day:" (Deuteronomy 8:11).

7. Your Heavenly Father Uses Crisis To Inspire Memory. "But thou shalt remember the Lord thy God: for it is He that giveth thee power to get wealth, that He may establish His covenant which He sware unto thy fathers, as it is this day" (Deuteronomy 8:18).

8. Jesus Loved Performing Miracles. "How God anointed Jesus of Nazareth with the Holy Ghost and with power: Who went about doing good, and healing all that were oppressed of the devil; for God was with Him" (Acts 10:38).

9. When Jesus Talked Each Word Was An Invitation To A Miracle.

The uncertain are invited to a miracle. Peter discovered this when Jesus invited him to walk on water. "And Peter answered Him and said, Lord, if it be Thou, bid me come unto Thee on the water. And He said, Come. And when Peter was come down out of the ship, he walked on the water, to go to Jesus" (Matthew 14:28,29).

The poor are invited to a miracle. "Give, and it shall be given unto you; good measure, pressed down, and shaken together, and running over, shall men give into your bosom. For with the same measure that ye mete withal it shall be measured to you again" (Luke 6:38).

The sick are invited to a miracle. The man who

had an infirmity for 38 years was invited to a miracle. "When Jesus saw him lie, and knew that he had been now a long time in that case, He saith unto him, Wilt thou be made whole?" (John 5:6).

12 Reminders About Miracles

1. Recognize That Any Assignment From God Will Require The Miracle Of God. You will not succeed alone.

2. Expect Miracles In Your Life Daily. "But without faith it is impossible to please Him: for he that cometh to God must believe that He is, and that He is a rewarder of them that diligently seek Him" (Hebrews 11:6).

3. Miracles Will Require A Continuous Flow Of Your Faith. "But without faith it is impossible to please Him: for he that cometh to God must believe that He is, and that He is a rewarder of them that diligently seek Him" (Hebrews 11:6).

4. Feed Your Faith Which Is Simply Your Confidence In God. It enters your heart when you *hear* the words of God *spoken*. "So then faith cometh by hearing, and hearing by the word of God" (Romans 10:17).

5. Understand That The Logic Of Your Mind And The Faith Of Your Heart Collide. They will wage war with each other continually. "For the flesh lusteth against the Spirit, and the Spirit against the flesh: and these are contrary the one to the other: so that ye cannot do the things that ye would. But the fruit of the Spirit is love, joy, peace, longsuffering, gentleness, goodness, faith," (Galatians 5:17,22).

6.   While Logic Produces Order, Faith Will Produce Miracles. God will *never* consult your *logic* to determine your future. He permits your *faith* to determine the levels of your promotion and victories. Logic is the wonderful and valuable gift He gives you to create order in your dealings with people.

7.   Faith Is The Wonderful And Valuable Gift He Gives You To Create Miracles...Through The Father.

8.   Your Assignment Will Require Miracle Relationships With Mentors, Protégés, Friends And Connections. For example, Joseph would never have gotten to the palace without the miracle relationship with the butler, a Divine Connection.

9.   Your Assignment May Require Supernatural Financial Provision. For example, Peter experienced the miracle of the coin in the mouth of the fish to pay taxes. Financial miracles are normal in the lives of those who obey God (see 1 Kings 17).

10. Your Assignment Will Require The Miracle Of Wisdom. Your decisions will open doors or close doors. Each decision you make will increase you or decrease you (see Proverbs 4:7).

11. Miracles Come Easily To The Obedient. "If ye be willing and obedient, ye shall eat the good of the land:" (Isaiah 1:19).

12. Any Move Toward Self-Sufficiency Is A Move Away From God. So cultivate continuous gratefulness and thankfulness in your heart for the presence of the Holy Spirit. Check His

God Never Reacts To Pain;
God Only Reacts To Pursuit.

-MIKE MURDOCK

countenance. Pursue His approval. "The Lord make His face shine upon thee, and be gracious unto thee: The Lord lift up His countenance upon thee, and give thee peace" (Numbers 6:25,26). "There be many that say, Who will shew us any good? Lord, lift Thou up the light of Thy countenance upon us" (Psalm 4:6). His countenance can be a very strong encouragement every moment of your life. "Why art thou cast down, O my soul? and why art thou disquieted in me? hope thou in God: for I shall yet praise Him for the help of His countenance" (Psalm 42:5).

Remember: *"Miracles Are Coming Toward You...Or Going Past You...Every Day Of Your Life"* (Oral Roberts).

Everything Good
Is Hated By
Everything Evil.

-MIKE MURDOCK

≈ 27 ≈

THE UNCOMMON FATHER ALWAYS KEEPS THE HEART OF A WARRIOR DURING EVERY SEASON OF BATTLE.

━━━━━◦━━━━━

Battle Is Inevitable.

The Uncommon Father knows this and refuses to lose heart. *Somebody will not like what he is doing. Ever.*

In the ancient writings of Ezra, a remarkable portrait is painted for us. When the foundation of the temple of the Lord was being laid, trumpets were sounded. They sang together by chorus in praising and giving thanks unto the Lord. Many of the priests wept and shouted for joy.

The noise was heard afar off. "And when the builders laid the foundation of the temple of the Lord, they set the priests in their apparel with trumpets, and the Levites the sons of Asaph with cymbals, to praise the Lord, after the ordinance of David king of Israel. And they sang together by course in praising and giving thanks unto the Lord; because He is good, for His mercy endureth for ever toward Israel. And all the people shouted with a great shout, when they praised the Lord, because the foundation of the house of the Lord was laid. But many of the priests and

The Size Of Your Enemy
Reveals How Big
God Sees You.

-MIKE MURDOCK

Levites and chief of the fathers, who were ancient men, that had seen the first house, when the foundation of this house was laid before their eyes, wept with a loud voice; and many shouted aloud for joy: So that the people could not discern the noise of the shout of joy from the noise of the weeping of the people: for the people shouted with a loud shout, and the noise was heard afar off" (Ezra 3:10-13).

Then, the attack began.

22 Defense Techniques To Remember During Seasons Of Battle

1.   Expect Someone To Be Unhappy Over Your Progress. They always are.   They "...hired counsellors against them, to frustrate their purpose, all the days of Cyrus king of Persia, even until the reign of Darius king of Persia" (Ezra 4:5). Letters were written. Accusations were believed.

Read it for yourself. "Now when the copy of king Artaxerxes' letter was read before Rehum, and Shimshai the scribe, and their companions, they went up in haste to Jerusalem unto the Jews, and made them to cease by force and power.   Then ceased the work of the house of God which is at Jerusalem. So it ceased unto the second year of the reign of Darius king of Persia" (Ezra 4:23,24).

2.   Remember That You Are A Champion, Not A Loser.

Champions Spend Their Time *Building* Their Dreams.

Losers Spend Their Lives *Criticizing* Those Dreams.

3.   Invest Your Words And Energy In Creating New Goals And Dreams. Losers invest their words and labor in trying to destroy the goals of others. "Let no corrupt communication proceed out of your mouth, but that which is good to the use of edifying, that it may minister grace unto the hearers. And grieve not the Holy Spirit of God, whereby ye are sealed unto the day of redemption. Let all bitterness, and wrath, and anger, and clamour, and evil speaking, be put away from you, with all malice:" (Ephesians 4:29-31).

4.   Recognize That What Makes You Weep May Cause Others To Become Angry. Nehemiah wept over the condition of Jerusalem. "And they said unto me, The remnant that are left of the captivity there in the province are in great affliction and reproach: the wall of Jerusalem also is broken down, and the gates thereof are burned with fire. And it came to pass, when I heard these words, that I sat down and wept, and mourned certain days, and fasted, and prayed before the God of heaven," (Nehemiah 1:3,4).

5.   Remember That When Your Assignment Is Awakened Within You, Your Adversary Is Awakened Against You.   It happened to Nehemiah.   "When Sanballat the Horonite, and Tobiah the servant, the Ammonite, heard of it, it grieved them exceedingly that there was come a man to seek the welfare of the children of Israel. But when Sanballat the Horonite, and Tobiah the servant, the Ammonite, and Geshem the Arabian, heard it, they laughed us to scorn, and despised us, and said, What is this thing that ye do?

will ye rebel against the king?" (Nehemiah 2:10,19). "But it came to pass, that when Sanballat, and Tobiah, and the Arabians, and the Ammonites, and the Ashdodites, heard that the walls of Jerusalem were made up, and that the breaches began to be stopped, then they were very wroth, And conspired all of them together to come and to fight against Jerusalem, and to hinder it" (Nehemiah 4:7,8).

6. Pray, Confess, Weep And Cast Yourself Down Before God. "Now when Ezra had prayed, and when he had confessed, weeping and casting himself down before the house of God, there assembled unto him out of Israel a very great congregation of men and women and children: for the people wept very sore" (Ezra 10:1).

7. Fast. Ezra did. "Then Ezra rose up from before the house of God, and went into the chamber of Johanan the son of Eliashib: and when he came thither, he did eat no bread, nor drink water: for he mourned because of the transgression of them that had been carried away" (Ezra 10:6).

8. Exhort Your Family To Be Strong And Unafraid, And To Be Willing To Fight For Their Families. Ezra did. "And I looked, and rose up, and said unto the nobles, and to the rulers, and to the rest of the people, Be not ye afraid of them: remember the Lord, which is great and terrible, and fight for your brethren, your sons, and your daughters, your wives, and your houses" (Nehemiah 4:14).

9. Stay Awake, Alert And Aware. Nehemiah did. "Nevertheless we made our prayer unto our God, and set a watch against them day and night, because of them" (Nehemiah 4:9; see also 1 Peter 5:8).

10. Stay Productive And Focused. Nehemiah did. "And it came to pass, when our enemies heard that it was known unto us, and God had brought their counsel to nought, that we returned all of us to the wall, every one unto his work" (Nehemiah 4:15).

11. Rearrange Your Daily Routine In Order To Be Cautious, Guarded And Protected From Your Enemies. Nehemiah did. "So neither I, nor my brethren, nor my servants, nor the men of the guard which followed me, none of us put off our clothes, saving that every one put them off for washing" (Nehemiah 4:23).

12. Encourage Singers And Spiritual Leaders Over You To Stay At Their Place Of Assignment. Nehemiah did. "Now it came to pass, when the wall was built, and I had set up the doors, and the porters and the singers and the Levites were appointed," (Nehemiah 7:1).

13. Secure The Leadership And Management Skills Of Faithful, Godly Mentors. Nehemiah did. "That I gave my brother Hanani, and Hananiah the ruler of the palace, charge over Jerusalem: for he was a faithful man, and feared God above many" (Nehemiah 7:2).

14. Study The Biographies Of Those Who Have Endured. Paul experienced much attack and criticism. "Alexander the coppersmith did me much evil: the Lord reward him according to his works: Of whom be thou ware also; for he hath greatly withstood our words" (2 Timothy 4:14,15).

15. Forgive Those Who Attack You, Knowing That God Will Stand With You. Paul did. When Paul experienced attack and alienation, he forgave and depended on the delivering power of God. "At my first answer no man stood with me, but all men forsook me: I pray God that it may not be laid to their charge. Notwithstanding the Lord stood with me, and strengthened me; that by me the preaching might be fully known, and that all the Gentiles might hear: and I was delivered out of the mouth of the lion" (2 Timothy 4:16,17).

16. Stay Focused On Your Assignment. Paul did. Paul stayed focused on the results of his ministry and kept his expectation on God as his deliverer. "And the Lord shall deliver me from every evil work, and will preserve me unto His heavenly kingdom: to Whom be glory for ever and ever. Amen." (2 Timothy 4:18).

17. Pursue The Presence Of God And His Word. David did. When David was attacked and criticized, he pursued the presence of God and absorbed the words of the covenant. "Unless Thy law had been my delights, I should then have perished in mine affliction" (Psalm 119:92).

18. Develop More Wisdom Regarding The Purpose Of Attack.

- ▶ Criticism is an observation designed to distract you.
- ▶ Attack is opposition designed to destroy you.
- ▶ Criticism is intended to demoralize you.
- ▶ Attack is intended to demoralize those around you, and anyone desiring to help you.

▶ Criticism is meant to make your future undesirable.

▶ Attack is to make your future unreachable.

▶ Critics will oppose your methods.

▶ Enemies oppose your motives.

19. Remember That Your Attitude Is More Important Than The Attack Against You. Attacks pass. Your attitude, if bitter or demoralized, can grow within you a root of bitterness that will poison every day of your future. "Looking diligently lest any man fail of the grace of God; lest any root of bitterness springing up trouble you, and thereby many be defiled;" (Hebrews 12:15).

20. Secure The Ministry Of Another Intercessor. "Again I say unto you, That if two of you shall agree on earth as touching any thing that they shall ask, it shall be done for them of My Father which is in heaven" (Matthew 18:19). This is why I write my Monthly Faith Partners regularly. I know the remarkable power of prayer partnership and the power of a prayer agreement (see Matthew 18:18,19).

21. Expect Your Faith To Be Honored Supernaturally By The God Who Intervenes... Just When You Need It The Most. "And Jesus answering saith unto them, Have faith in God. For verily I say unto you, That whosoever shall say unto this mountain, Be thou removed, and be thou cast into the sea; and shall not doubt in his heart, but shall believe that those things which he saith shall come to pass; he shall have whatsoever he saith. Therefore I say unto you, What things soever ye desire, when ye pray, believe that ye receive them, and ye shall have them" (Mark 11:22-24).

The Mistakes Of Your Adversary
Are Simply
The Miracles Of Your God.

-MIKE MURDOCK

22. Expect God To Bring The Counsel Of Your Enemies To Nought. "And it came to pass, when our enemies heard that it was known unto us, and God had brought their counsel to nought, that we returned all of us to the wall, every one unto His work" (Nehemiah 4:15).

≈ 28 ≈

THE UNCOMMON FATHER VIEWS EVERY CRISIS AS THE GOLDEN GATE TO A MIRACLE.

➤➤-◉-≪◀

Crisis Never Surprises God.
Crisis is normal to the Uncommon Father.

Peter believed this. "Beloved, think it not strange concerning the fiery trial which is to try you, as though some strange thing happened unto you: But rejoice, inasmuch as ye are partakers of Christ's sufferings; that, when His glory shall be revealed, ye may be glad also with exceeding joy" (1 Peter 4:12,13).

20 Important Facts Every Father Should Remember During Crisis Times

1. **Every Champion In Scripture Seemed To Move Continually From One Crisis Into Another.** "But in all things approving ourselves as the ministers of God, in much patience, in afflictions, in necessities, in distresses, In stripes, in imprisonments, in tumults, in labours, in watchings, in fastings;" (2 Corinthians 6:4,5).

2. **Paul Experienced Highs And Lows In Favor And Disfavor.** "By honour and dishonour, by evil report and good report: as deceivers, and yet true; As unknown, and yet well known; as dying, and,

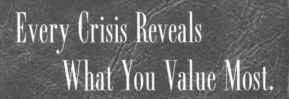

Every Crisis Reveals
What You Value Most.

-MIKE MURDOCK

behold, we live; as chastened, and not killed; As sorrowful, yet alway rejoicing; as poor, yet making many rich; as having nothing, and yet possessing all things" (2 Corinthians 6:8-10).

3.   Jesus Experienced Numerous Crises. It finally seemed to end at the crucifixion. Yet even at His crucifixion, He was jeered and taunted by His enemies. Even His resurrection has been doubted by thousands (read Matthew 27:40-43).

4.   Crisis Is Simply The Golden Hinge On The Door Of Promotion. Every Champion has had difficult circumstances to overcome.

> ► *Daniel* experienced being thrown into the *lions' den.*
> ► *Three Hebrew children* experienced the *fiery furnace.*
> ► *Job* experienced a *total loss* of children, possessions and good health.
> ► *Elijah* had his brook *dry up.*
> ► *The widow of Zarephath* came to her last meal during the famine, almost starving.
> ► *Joseph* experienced hatred by his brothers, *false accusation against his character,* and then was forgotten in prison two years after he interpreted the dream of the butler.
> ► *Isaac* had one foolish son, Esau, and a deceptive, manipulative son called Jacob.

A visit to a workshop would benefit us. Picture this scenario. Pause for a moment and revisit the workshop where a world-renowned missionary evangelist is speaking. The place is crammed with young preachers who are excited about the revelation imparted through this man. When you walk through the door, you are looking for a tall, good-looking and powerfully built man with exquisite stature and dynamic magnetism. You ask for him, and they point to a squinty eyed, short, bowlegged man speaking from the platform.

Listen to him. "Are they ministers of Christ? (I speak as a fool) I am more; in labours more abundant, in stripes above measure, in prisons more frequent, in deaths oft. Of the Jews five times received I forty stripes save one. Thrice was I beaten with rods, once was I stoned, thrice I suffered shipwreck, a night and a day I have been in the deep; In journeyings often, in perils of waters, in perils of robbers, in perils by mine own countrymen, in perils by the heathen, in perils in the city, in perils in the wilderness, in perils in the sea, in perils among false brethren; In weariness and painfulness, in watchings often, in hunger and thirst, in fastings often, in cold and nakedness. Beside those things that are without, that which cometh upon me daily, the care of all the churches. Who is weak, and I am not weak? who is offended, and I burn not?" (2 Corinthians 11:23-29).

Paul is not complaining. He is exultant! "If I must needs glory, I will glory of the things which concern mine infirmities" (2 Corinthians 11:30).

5. Remember That Crisis Attracts The Power And Strength Of God. Paul wrote, "And He said unto me, My grace is sufficient for thee: for My strength is made perfect in weakness. Most gladly therefore will I rather glory in my infirmities, that the power of Christ may rest upon me. Therefore I take pleasure in infirmities, in reproaches, in necessities, in persecutions, in distresses for Christ's sake: for when I am weak, then am I strong" (2 Corinthians 12:9,10).

6. Uncommon Fathers Embrace The Season Of Crisis As A Passage. "If we suffer, we shall also reign with Him: if we deny Him, He also will deny us:" (2 Timothy 2:12). "And if children, then heirs; heirs of God, and joint-heirs with Christ; if so be that we suffer with Him, that we may be also glorified together. For I reckon that the sufferings of this present time are not worthy to be compared with the glory which shall be revealed in us" (Romans 8:17,18).

7. Anticipate Recognition And Reward For Surviving The Crisis. His voice was filled with energy, excitement and joy. "I have fought a good fight, I have finished my course, I have kept the faith: Henceforth there is laid up for me a crown of righteousness, which the Lord, the righteous judge, shall give me at that day: and not to me only, but unto all them also that love His appearing" (2 Timothy 4:7,8).

8. Remember When Your Own Difficult Days Were Caused By Ignorance Instead Of The Birthing Of Promotion. "For we ourselves also were sometimes foolish, disobedient, deceived, serving divers lusts and pleasures, living in malice and envy, hateful, and hating one another. But after that the kindness and love of God our Saviour toward man appeared, Not by works of righteousness which we have done, but according to His mercy He saved us, by the washing of regeneration, and renewing of the Holy Ghost; Which He shed on us abundantly through Jesus Christ our Saviour; That being justified by His grace, we should be made heirs

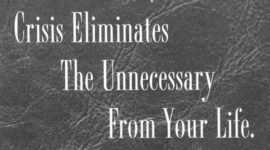

Crisis Eliminates
The Unnecessary
From Your Life.

-MIKE MURDOCK

according to the hope of eternal life" (Titus 3:3-7).

9.   Look Beyond The Present Crisis. The Apostle Paul wrote. "Looking for that blessed hope, and the glorious appearing of the great God and our Saviour Jesus Christ;" (Titus 2:13).

10.   Focus What Is On The Other Side Of Suffering And Crisis. Peter did. "But rejoice, inasmuch as ye are partakers of Christ's sufferings; that, when His glory shall be revealed, ye may be glad also with exceeding joy. If ye be reproached for the name of Christ, happy are ye; for the spirit of glory and of God resteth upon you: on their part He is evil spoken of, but on your part He is glorified" (1 Peter 4:13,14).

11.   Imagine The Crown Of Life That Awaits Beyond Crisis. James did. "Blessed is the man that endureth temptation: for when he is tried, he shall receive the crown of life, which the Lord hath promised to them that love Him" (James 1:12).

12.   Expect Your Crisis To Produce Patience. "Knowing this, that the trying of your faith worketh patience" (James 1:3).

13.   Expect Your Patience To Produce Every Miracle And Desired Provision You Could Want. "But let patience have her perfect work, that ye may be perfect and entire, wanting nothing" (James 1:4).

14.   Acknowledge The Holy Spirit As Your Companion Through Every Crisis. "But now thus saith the Lord that created thee, O Jacob, and He that formed thee, O Israel, Fear not: for I have redeemed thee, I have called thee by thy name; thou art Mine. When thou passest through the waters, I will be with

When You Ask God
For A Future
He Schedules An
Adversary To
Authorize Your Promotion.

-MIKE MURDOCK

thee; and through the rivers, they shall not overflow thee: when thou walkest through the fire, thou shalt not be burned; neither shall the flame kindle upon thee" (Isaiah 43:1,2).

15. Rest In The Promise That Your Crisis Will Pass. "For His anger endureth but a moment; in His favour is life: weeping may endure for a night, but joy cometh in the morning" (Psalm 30:5).

16. Keep Discussing The Rewards Beyond Crisis. "Now no chastening for the present seemeth to be joyous, but grievous: nevertheless afterward it yieldeth the peaceable fruit of righteousness unto them which are exercised thereby. Wherefore lift up the hands which hang down, and the feeble knees; And make straight paths for your feet, lest that which is lame be turned out of the way; but let it rather be healed" (Hebrews 12:11-13).

17. Never Discuss The Problems Of Your Crisis With Anyone Incapable Of Solving Them. "A fool uttereth all his mind: but a wise man keepeth it in till afterwards" (Proverbs 29:11).

18. Expect To Learn More In Crisis Than You Will Ever Learn In Any Victory. "Though He were a Son, yet learned He obedience by the things which He suffered;" (Hebrews 5:8).

19. View Crisis As The Season In Which God Has An Opportunity To Reveal His Love And Supernatural Power To Your Life. "And He said unto me, My grace is sufficient for thee: for My strength is made perfect in weakness. Most gladly therefore will I rather glory in my infirmities, that the power of Christ may rest upon me. Therefore I take pleasure in infirmities, in reproaches, in necessities, in persecutions, in distresses for Christ's sake: for when I am weak, then am I strong" (2 Corinthians 12:9,10).

20. Increase Your Time Spent In "The Secret Place." Your Prayer Closet Will Bring Protection. "For in the time of trouble He shall hide me in His pavilion: in the secret of His tabernacle shall He hide me; He shall set me up upon a rock. And now shall mine head be lifted up above mine enemies round about me: therefore will I offer in His tabernacle sacrifices of joy; I will sing, yea, I will sing praises unto the Lord" (Psalm 27:5,6).

Crisis Is Always An Exit From Your Present.

Crisis Is Your Passage To Promotion.

Remember: *Crisis Is A Normal Event On The Road To Your Assignment.*

❧ 29 ❧

THE UNCOMMON FATHER FEELS THE PAIN OF THOSE WHO HURT AROUND HIM.

The Whole Earth Hurts.

Paul explained it, "For we know that the whole creation groaneth and travaileth in pain together until now" (Romans 8:22).

True compassion feels the pain by those around it...the pure heart knows and responds.

The Uncommon Father knows his Assignment will always be to someone who is hurting.

3 Facts About The Healing Power Of Jesus

1.   **Jesus Came To Heal And Restore.** "The thief cometh not, but for to steal, and to kill, and to destroy: I am come that they might have life, and that they might have it more abundantly" (John 10:10).

"How God anointed Jesus of Nazareth with the Holy Ghost and with power: Who went about doing good, and healing all that were oppressed of the devil; for God was with him" (Acts 10:38).

2.   **Jesus Commanded The Disciples To Heal And Restore.** "Heal the sick, cleanse the lepers, raise the dead, cast out devils: freely ye have

Those Who Unlock
    Your Compassion Are
Those To Whom You
    Have Been Assigned.

-MIKE MURDOCK

received, freely give" (Matthew 10:8).

3. Jesus Expects You To Heal And Restore. "For I was an hungred, and ye gave me meat: I was thirsty, and ye gave me drink: I was a stranger, and ye took me in: Naked, and ye clothed me: I was sick, and ye visited me: I was in prison, and ye came unto me" (Matthew 25:35,36).

The whole world is still hurting, and *somebody, somewhere, is waiting for you.*

5 Ways To Recognize When Your Family Qualifies To Receive From You

1. They Must Recognize Their Need. They must have the humility to *admit* they are wounded. "I know thy works, that thou art neither cold nor hot: I would thou wert cold or hot. So then because thou art lukewarm, and neither cold nor hot, I will spue thee out of My mouth. Because thou sayest, I am rich, and increased with goods, and have need of nothing; and knowest not that thou art wretched, and miserable, and poor, and blind, and naked:" (Revelation 3:15-17). You see, many people permit their pride to isolate them from the hand of God.

That is why Jesus said, "And Jesus answering said unto them, They that are whole need not a physician; but they that are sick. I came not to call the righteous, but sinners to repentance" (Luke 5:31,32).

The Unrepentant Are Disqualified To Receive Help.

2. Your Family Should Believe In Your

The Reward For Repentance Is The Ability To Change.

-MIKE MURDOCK

Competence, Knowledge And Motive. They must have full confidence that you are assigned by God in their season of hurt. "O Jerusalem, Jerusalem, thou that killest the prophets, and stonest them which are sent unto thee, how often would I have gathered thy children together, even as a hen gathereth her chickens under her wings, and ye would not! Behold, your house is left unto you desolate. For I say unto you, Ye shall not see me henceforth, till ye shall say, Blessed is he that cometh in the name of the Lord" (Matthew 23:37-39).

Jesus Himself could not heal Israel because they did not see Him as the Son of God. They refused to recognize His divinity. "And they were offended in Him. But Jesus said unto them, A prophet is not without honour, save in his own country, and in his own house" (Matthew 13:57).

This is a troubling experience.

Some of my own relatives and close friends have needed assistance from time to time. Sometimes, the Holy Spirit has *stopped* me from reaching out. When I ask why, He reminds me that: 1) they have *refused mentorship—even refused to attend* special conferences I have sponsored that would have solved their problems; 2) they have *refused to read* books or *listen* to tapes that answer every question they have asked; and 3) they have *not followed previous counsel* I have given them in countless conversations.

3. Your Family Should Pursue And Reach For Your Involvement And Counsel. *Asking* begins the receiving process. They must be willing to take immediate action and respond. The ministry of Jesus succeeded in the hearts of those who

Those Who Refuse To Trust
Become Incapable
Of Change.

-MIKE MURDOCK

reached. "And when the men of that place had knowledge of Him, they sent out into all that country round about, and brought unto Him all that were diseased; And besought Him that they might only touch the hem of His garment: and as many as touched were made perfectly whole" (Matthew 14:35,36).

4.   Your Family Should Cooperate With Your Advice. They must be willing to pay the price of persistence to cooperate with your schedule and availability.   You see, you are not necessarily needing them—*they need you.*   When great men seriously wanted the help of Christ they came to Him *wherever He was.*   "Can two walk together except they be agreed?" (Amos 3:3).

5.   Your   Family   Should   Persist Regardless Of Their Discomfort. "And, behold, a woman of Canaan came out of the same coasts, and cried unto Him, saying, Have mercy on me, O Lord, Thou Son of David; my daughter is grievously vexed with a devil. *But He answered her not a word.* And His disciples came and besought Him, saying, Send her away; for she crieth after us" (Matthew 15:22,23). *Note this: Jesus refused to respond.* Why? We really do not know other than His answer a few sentences later. "But He answered her not a word. And His disciples came and besought Him, saying, Send her away; for she crieth after us. But He answered and said, I am not sent but unto the lost sheep of the house of Israel. Then came she and worshipped Him, saying, Lord, help me" (verses 23-25).

She asked.

Jesus ignored.

She worshipped.

Jesus *responded.*

"But He answered and said, It is not meet to take the children's bread, and to cast it to dogs. And she said, Truth, Lord: yet the dogs eat of the crumbs which fall from their masters' table. Then Jesus answered and said unto her, O woman, great is thy faith: be it unto thee even as thou wilt. And her daughter was made whole from that very hour" (Matthew 15:26-28).

There is a *reason* God left this story in the Bible for you.

Her *asking* did not move Jesus.

Her *worship* moved Him.

Her *appreciation* stirred Him.

Her *persistence* qualified her.

These Are The Qualities That Qualify Your Family To Receive From You.

Father, remember: *Your Assignment Will Always Be To Someone Who Is Hurting...*and they are often those *in your own house.*

～ 30 ～

THE UNCOMMON FATHER IS THE MASTER PROBLEM-SOLVER IN HIS HOME.

➣━●━≪

Everything Created Is A Solution To A Problem.

Your Assignment will always be to someone with a problem.

The Uncommon Father knows he contains the answers for the problem situation around him. He is the Burden-Bearer, not the burden in his home.

John, the beloved disciple, urged compassion for those hurting around us. "But whoso hath this world's good, and seeth his brother have need, and shutteth up his bowels of compassion from him, how dwelleth the love of God in him?" (1 John 3:17).

14 Principles In Problem Solving You Must Recognize And Apply When Helping Others

1.   **Your Family Needs You.** *Especially when they have a problem.*

▶ Somebody with a health problem needs a doctor.

▶ Somebody with a car problem needs a mechanic.

▶ Somebody with financial problems needs a banker.

Your Rewards In Life
Are Determined
By The Problems You
Are Willing To Solve
For Others.

-MIKE MURDOCK

▶ Somebody with a spiritual problem needs a minister.

Problems...*are really wonderful things.*

Problems...make us *reach for each other.*

Problems...enable us to *discern the value* of others.

Problems...enable others to *discern our difference,* too. So *never* run from a problem. Simply *run toward the solution.*

2. Some Problems Will Be More Noticeable Than Others. Tailors notice missing buttons. Mechanics *hear* something wrong in car engines. Why? That is their specific Assignment.

3. God Expects You To Move Swiftly To Solve A Problem For Those To Whom You Are Assigned. "Withhold not good from them to whom it is due, when it is in the power of thine hand to do it" (Proverbs 3:27).

4. Your Assignment Will Determine And Heighten What You See And Hear. You will see things others close to you do not notice. You will *hear* things in a conversation that others may overlook. *The problem you notice* is a clue to your anointing and calling in life.

5. You Are Not Assigned To Everybody With A Problem. Some problems are impossible for *you* to solve. Somebody else has been assigned to solve *those specific problems* for people. However, you must learn to stay in the *center of your expertise,* the solutions *you* contain.

6. The Holy Spirit Will Answer Every Important Question You Ask. His answers will bring great peace to your heart. "Call unto Me, and I will answer thee, and shew thee great and mighty things, which thou knowest not" (Jeremiah 33:3).

a. *Ask Him Honestly If The Problem You Are Seeing Is The Penalty For An Act Of Disobedience Or Rebellion.* Why?

Never Breathe Life Into Something God Is Killing.

The last thing you want to do is oppose the workings of God in the life of someone.

Let me explain. Recently, someone was discussing her son with me. She said, "I feel so sorry for him. He has been out of work for several months. So I have been giving him spending money and letting him stay at the house. Could you help him in some way?"

Further discussion revealed that the young man was unbelievably lazy. He had presented no resumes to any companies. He had *refused* to do small chores around the house. He had not even mowed the grass at his mother's home, nor washed and waxed her car during the days he was "out of work."

I refused to help the young man and encouraged her to *withdraw* her support. I explained Deuteronomy 28, where God said He would only "bless the work of our hands." Paul wrote to the church at Thessalonica, "For even when we were with you, this we commanded you, that if any would not work, neither should he eat. For we hear that there are some which walk among you disorderly, working not at all, but are busybodies" (2 Thessalonians 3:10,11).

The Bible says you should withdraw from lazy people. Part from them. "And if any man obey not our word by this epistle, note that man, and have no company with him, that he may be ashamed" (2 Thessalonians 3:14).

Now, he is *not* an enemy. He is a *brother. But* he must be taught the *law of productivity:* Increase requires work.

b. *Ask The Holy Spirit.* "Is this person having a problem due to ignorance? Am I assigned to *teach* him?" You see, this is what Philip did when he ran to the Ethiopian eunuch and asked, "And Philip ran thither to him, and heard him read the prophet Esaias, and said, Understandest thou what thou readest?" (Acts 8:30). Now, the eunuch was not learned, but he *wanted to be taught!* Philip did not have to force him to become a student. "And he said, How can I, except some man should guide me? And he desired Philip that he would come up and sit with him" (Acts 8:31).

c. *Ask The Holy Spirit,* "Am I the one You have *assigned* to solve this problem for this person?" *If* you are, great joy will enter you as you bond with this person to find a solution to his problem. This is why the Scripture emphasizes in Proverbs 3:27, "Withhold not good from them *to whom it is due."*

d. *Ask The Holy Spirit,* "Have You qualified *me* to solve *this* problem and is this *the right time* to do so?" You see, the Scriptures instruct to solve a problem *"when it is in the power of thine hand to do it"* (Proverbs 3:27).

I often see many problems I want to solve. But the Holy Spirit *forbids* me. I do not always know why. But He has a specific plan. Paul experienced this also. "Now when they had gone throughout Phrygia

God Does Not Always
    Call The Qualified;
But He Always Qualifies
    The Called.

-MIKE MURDOCK

and the region of Galatia, and *were forbidden of the Holy Ghost* to preach the word in Asia, After they were come to Mysia, they assayed to go into Bithynia: *but the Spirit suffered them not"* (Acts 16:6,7).

7. Accept That The Holy Spirit Will Sometimes Forbid You To Solve A Problem For Someone. It would seem that the gospel preached by Paul would solve a problem for everybody, everywhere he went. But God always has a plan.

He has *reasons.*

He has *seasons.*

"To every thing there is a season, and a time to every purpose under the heaven: A time to be born, and a time to die; a time to plant, and a time to pluck up that which is planted; A time to kill, and a time to heal; a time to break down, and a time to build up;" (Ecclesiastes 3:1-3).

8. Stay Aware That The Attitude Of The Person With The Problem Is More Important To God Than The Problem They Are Facing. You see, a rebel is not in position to receive from the Lord. But, "If ye be willing and obedient, ye shall eat the good of the land:" (Isaiah 1:19).

Timing is so vital to the Holy Spirit. Permit Him to direct your steps in this area *every single day* of your life. "Behold, I stand at the door, and knock: if any man hear My voice, and open the door, I will come in to him, and will sup with him, and he with Me" (Revelation 3:20).

9. God Will Give You Supernatural Compassion For The Person With The Problem.

10. God Will Provide You With Understanding And Time To Respond Properly To The

Weakness Is Always
The Catalyst
For The Pursuit Of God.

-MIKE MURDOCK

Problem (see Genesis 41:15-36).

11. The Person Will Have Great Confidence In Your Ability And Calling To Solve The Problem For Them (see Acts 8:31-39 and Genesis 41:37-42).

12. God Will Confirm Your Assignment With Inner Peace In You, And With Joy In Them (see Genesis 41:15-44 and Acts 8:31-39).

13. Your Assignment Will Always Be At A Critical Turning Point In That Person's Life (see Acts 8:31-39 and Genesis 41:15-44).

14. Your Assignment Will Never Take You Away From Your Time With The Holy Spirit And Private Prayer. "But seek ye first the kingdom of God, and His righteousness; and all these things shall be added unto you" (Matthew 6:33).

Emergencies that take you out of His presence and out of your time spent with God are usually orchestrated by hell *to break the rhythm of your spiritual life.*

Every pastor receives "emergency phone calls" that come just before his preaching service. It is intended to *break his focus.* Be ruthless with deadly distractions.

The Uncommon Father Depends On The Holy Spirit To Qualify Him To Solve Any Problem You Face

God Made A Wise Decision When He Chose You.
God is not stupid. He is brilliant; He is aware; He is knowledgeable. *He does things that men would never do.* "But now thus saith the Lord that created

thee, O Jacob, and He that formed thee, O Israel, Fear not: for I have redeemed thee, I have called thee by thy name; thou art Mine" (Isaiah 43:1).

If you were incapable, He would not have placed this burning desire in you.

13 Mental Battles Every Father May Face

1.   You May Feel Incapable. "And Moses said unto God, Who am I, that I should go unto Pharaoh, and that I should bring forth the children of Israel out of Egypt?" (Exodus 3:11).

2.   You May Feel Weak And Inarticulate. "And I was with you in weakness, and in fear, and in much trembling. And my speech and my preaching was not with enticing words of man's wisdom, but in demonstration of the Spirit and of power:" (1 Corinthians 2:3,4).

3.   You May Feel Unworthy. "Whereof I was made a minister, according to the gift of the grace of God given unto me by the effectual working of His power. Unto me, who am less than the least of all saints, is this grace given, that I should preach among the Gentiles the unsearchable riches of Christ;" (Ephesians 3:7,8).

4.   You May Feel Foolish And Weak. "But God hath chosen the foolish things of the world to confound the wise; and God hath chosen the weak things of the world to confound the things which are mighty;" (1 Corinthians 1:27).

5.   You May Feel Despised And Undesired By Anyone.   "And base things of the world, and things which are despised, hath God chosen, yea, and things which are not, to bring to nought things that are: That no flesh should glory in His presence" (1 Corinthians 1:28,29).

6. You May Feel Powerless, Without Clout And Influence. "For Thou, Lord, wilt bless the righteous; with favour wilt Thou compass him as with a shield" (Psalm 5:12).

7. You May Feel Unspiritual And Carnal. Listen to Paul: "This is a faithful saying, and worthy of all acceptation, that Christ Jesus came into the world to save sinners; of whom I am chief. Howbeit for this cause I obtained mercy, that in me first Jesus Christ might shew forth all longsuffering, for a pattern to them which should hereafter believe on Him to life everlasting" (1 Timothy 1:15,16).

8. You May Feel Ignorant, Or That You Have A Blemished Past. "And I thank Christ Jesus our Lord, Who hath enabled me, for that He counted me faithful, putting me into the ministry; Who was before a blasphemer, and a persecutor, and injurious: but I obtained mercy, because I did it ignorantly in unbelief. And the grace of our Lord was exceeding abundant with faith and love which is in Christ Jesus" (1 Timothy 1:12-14).

9. You May Feel Defenseless. "My defence is of God, which saveth the upright in heart" (Psalm 7:10).

10. You May Feel That You Have Too Many Enemies. "When mine enemies are turned back, they shall fall and perish at Thy presence. For Thou hast maintained my right and my cause; Thou satest in the throne judging right" (Psalm 9:3,4).

11. You May Feel Too Needy. "For the needy shall not alway be forgotten: the expectation of the poor shall not perish for ever" (Psalm 9:18).

12. You May Feel That It Will Take Too Long For God To Assist You And To Help You Become What You Are Supposed To Be. "God is our refuge and strength, a very present help in trouble" (Psalm 46:1). "God is in the midst of her; she shall not be moved: God shall help her, and that right early" (Psalm 46:5).

13. You May Feel Overwhelmed By Adversity. "Through Thee will we push down our enemies: through Thy name will we tread them under that rise up against us" (Psalm 44:5).

God is not looking at your *outward* appearance. He is looking at *your heart.* Keep it pure before Him. Pursue Him daily and with great diligence. And speak this great promise aloud throughout today: "I can do all things through Christ which strengtheneth me" (Philippians 4:13).

Ten Commandments For The Uncommon Father

1. Fully Embrace Every Season Of Divine Preparation. "Study to shew thyself approved unto God, a workman that needeth not to be ashamed, rightly dividing the word of truth" (2 Timothy 2:15).

2. Determine To Persevere Through Seasons Of Solitude And Isolation From Others. "Study to shew thyself approved unto God, a workman that needeth not to be ashamed, rightly dividing the word of truth" (2 Timothy 2:15).

3.   Refuse To Discuss Your Assignment With Scorners And Fools. "Go from the presence of a foolish man, when thou perceivest not in him the lips of knowledge" (Proverbs 14:7).

4.   Be Willing To Work Diligently And Become Qualified.   "The soul of the sluggard desireth, and hath nothing: but the soul of the diligent shall be made fat" (Proverbs 13:4).

5.   Be Very Discreet About Your Personal Plans. "He that keepeth his mouth keepeth his life: but he that openeth wide his lips shall have destruction" (Proverbs 13:3).

6.   Expect God To Hear Your Prayers. "The Lord is far from the wicked: but He heareth the prayer of the righteous" (Proverbs 15:29).

7.   Seek Correction And Direction From Worthy Mentors. "The ear that heareth the reproof of life abideth among the wise. He that refuseth instruction despiseth his own soul: but he that heareth reproof getteth understanding" (Proverbs 15:31,32).

8.   Expect Unnecessary Conflict To Be Avoided. "When a man's ways please the Lord, He maketh even his enemies to be at peace with him. (Proverbs 16:7).

9.   Appreciate The Finances God Has Presently Provided, And Expect Him To Provide Supernaturally, On His Schedule. "Better is a little with righteousness than great revenues without right" (Proverbs 16:8). "But my God shall supply all your need according to His riches in

The Presence Of God
Is The Only Place
Your Weakness Will Die.

-*MIKE MURDOCK*

glory by Christ Jesus" (Philippians 4:19).

10. Expect The Gifts Of God Within You To Open Unexpected Doors Of Opportunity. "A man's gift maketh room for him, and bringeth him before great men" (Proverbs 18:16).

I wrote a song several years ago:

"He does not always call the qualified,
But He qualifies the called!
So, you can! You can!"

In His presence, you *become* qualified.

Father, remember: The Holy Spirit Will Qualify You To Solve Any Problem You Face In Your Home.

The Only Reason
Men Fail Is
Broken Focus.

-MIKE MURDOCK

❧ 31 ❧

THE UNCOMMON FATHER DISCERNS DISTRACTIONS AND OVERCOMES THEM.

Distractions Are Deadly.

The Uncommon Father refuses four kinds of people who distract him from his life Assignment.

Conversations can birth tragedies. Ask Adam and Eve about their little talk with the serpent in the Garden of Eden.

Even intimacy can destroy.

Intimacy with one wrong person can destroy you forever.

▶ When God Wants To Promote You, He Puts A *Person* In Your Life.

▶ When Satan Wants To Destroy You, He Places A Person *Close To You.*

5 Kinds Of Distractions

1. **Those Who Do Not Really Accept Your Assignment Of Fatherhood.** They do not really know you. They have not spent time with God, *fasting and praying for you.* Usually, they look on the outward appearance of you and your circumstances. They laugh at your dreams and goals.

I have a precious friend who is well along in

years. He is a white-haired fireball of energy. When God spoke to him to birth a church in a new city, some folks laughed. He had been a businessman. *But he knew the Voice of God.* Those who refused to accept his Assignment as from the Lord *refused to participate.* Now, he is a very successful pastor and is doing a great work for God. Had he listened to those who had never consulted the Holy Spirit in the first place, he might have been a total failure today.

4 Questions To Qualify People For Access Or Friendship

▶ *Have They Taken The Time To Pray Privately About Your Vision And Goal?*
▶ *Have They Questioned You At Length To Develop A Full Understanding Of Your Assignment?*
▶ *How Many Hours Have You Really Spent With Them?*
▶ *Are They Willing To Pray With You And Walk Side By Side With You Concerning Your Assignment?*

2. **Those Who Do Not Truly Respect Your Assignment As Divine.** I must tell you this personal illustration. I really believe every person should have a life product, a life legacy. For example, furniture companies produce furniture. Piano companies produce pianos. Sign companies produce signs. An automobile company produces automobiles. You should know *the legacy God has designed for you to leave upon earth*—your Assignment.

So I asked my precious mother, "Mother, what is

your life product?"

"Oh son, I do not have any life product. I am just trying to get you seven kids to heaven."

Now that truly is a life product—the salvation and redemption of your seven children!

Some people have criticized my mother because she had dedicated her entire life to being a wife to my father, and a full-time mother at home. I have heard many words over the years as people said, "You need to get out of this house and away from these kids and get yourself a job!"

Those people have little respect for mothers, housewives and those *who are called alongside their husbands.* How I thank God that my mother refused their influence! My memories of home are of *constant and total access to my mother and father.* They had family altar times *twice a day,* morning and night. Mother enforced *memorization* of one Scripture each morning. I believe that my own Assignment became defined, refined and confined *because of a mother who respected her own Assignment.*

Recently, a pastor of a large well-known church asked me, "Mike, I wish you would not hold crusades at these small little churches around town here. My people like to feel that our church is so successful that we can attract international ministries others cannot schedule. It would mean a lot to me if you would come to just my church when you come to this city." He had little respect for ministers with small congregations. This kind of attitude is sad.

3.   **Those Who Have Little Respect Refuse To Invest In Your Assignment.** They may even

When Wrong People
Leave Your Life
Right Things
Start Happening.

-MIKE MURDOCK

claim to love you, but they do not respect your Assignment. Let me explain. I host a major World Wisdom Conference each year. It costs thousands of dollars for me to sponsor it. I fly in some of the most effective ministers who have ever spoken. It is first-class all the way. Yet some people live 30 minutes away and will not even drive over to the Conference for one day. I have relatives and close family members who will not come for just one day. It is the focus of my entire year, but they have *little respect for Wisdom,* the anointing or my ministry. Now, I cannot say they do not love me. But, *they refuse to invest in this anointing and flow of Wisdom.*

Love Is Viewing Someone As *Desirable.*

Respect Is Viewing Someone As *Valuable.*

Never Linger In The Presence Of Those Who Do Not Respect Your Assignment. People will never *protect* what they do not *respect.*

4. Those Who Will Not Protect Your Assignment Through Their Discretion. What You Respect, You Will *Protect.* I have known hundreds of men of God during my 58 years on earth. Some are well-known, effective and have done an incredible work for God. Yes, I have observed their weaknesses, flaws and human traits. It has endeared me to them, not alienated me from them. *I have refused to discuss those flaws with anyone.* Why? It is the right thing to do in the eyes of God...and I want others to show mercy to me, too!

Have you ever read the complete story of David and how he protected the position and calling of Saul? He refused to damage and destroy the influence of Saul, though Saul's actions were foolish and devastating. He even tried to kill David and his own son, Jonathan (David's closest friend).

Yet the discretion and loyalty of David became legendary. An entire nation saw a man of integrity, honor, graciousness and dignity. He was not condoning the behavior and conduct of a fool. Rather, *he respected the Assignment of Saul.*

Years later, when David was brokenhearted, his mind was aflame with memories of the water at Bethlehem. He wished for it aloud. One of his thoughts of longing was, "And David longed, and said, Oh that one would give me drink of the water of the well of Bethlehem, which is by the gate!" (2 Samuel 23:15). His three strongest leaders broke through the host of the Philistines and brought him back water. He refused to drink it because it involved the life of his own men that he loved. That kind of loyalty was inspired because David protected the anointing, the mantle and the Assignment *of another.* In time, his own men had *developed a protection* for his Assignment.

One of my close friends had a drug problem. It concerned me deeply. Even though he refused to face it honestly, I refused to advertise his problem. Why? I wanted to protect his Assignment. His life is not over. His future is not ended. God *still* has His hand on his life. As I protect that Assignment within him, God will honor and bless my own ministry for it.

Move Away From Wrong People Who Will Not Protect Your Name, Your Focus And Your Calling. Look at Samson. Watch the conniving, scheming and manipulation of Delilah as she sought to probe for his area of weakness.

Wrong People Breathe Life Into Your Weakness.
Right People Starve Your Weakness.

5.   Those Who Do Not Expect You To Really Achieve Your Assignment. They have little faith in you. Remember Eliab, the oldest brother of David who acted angrily when David discussed killing the lion?

Eliab reacted angrily toward David. "And Eliab his eldest brother heard when he spake unto the men; and Eliab's anger was kindled against David, and he said, Why camest thou down hither? and with whom hast thou left those few sheep in the wilderness? I know thy pride, and the naughtiness of thine heart; for thou art come down that thou mightest see the battle" (1 Samuel 17:28).

His own family saw him as a little shepherd boy, *unaware of his victories* over the lion and bear. They *expected* him to fail. They could not imagine him on the throne. He was their "baby brother."

Do you have someone in your family who feels the same way about your life and future? *Do not waste your energy* and time attempting to persuade them. God will vindicate you.

4 Reminders For The Uncommon Father

1.   Time Will Validate You. "And let us not be weary in well doing: for in due season we shall reap, if we faint not" (Galatians 6:9).

2.   Keep Solving Problems. Stay alive and vibrant.

3.   Keep Your Spirit Sweet. And permit God to do the *promoting*. "As we have therefore opportunity, let us do good unto all men, especially

unto them who are of the household of faith"
(Galatians 6:10).

    4. **People Are Merely Channels; They Are
Not Your Source.** "For promotion cometh neither
from the east, nor from the west, nor from the south.
But God is the judge: He putteth down one, and
setteth up another" (Psalm 75:6,7).

7 Important Reminders For Relationships

    1. **Intimacy Should Be Earned, Not
Freely Given** (read 1 Thessalonians 5:12,13).

    2. **Intimacy Should Be The Reward For
Proven Loyalty** (read John 15:13,14).

    3. **True Friendship Is A Gift, Never A
Demanded Requirement** (read 1 Corinthians 13).

    4. **When Wrong People Leave Your Life,
Wrong Things Stop Happening** (read Jonah 1:15).

    5. **When Right People Enter Your Life,
Right Things Begin To Happen** (read John 4:4-30).

    6. **If You Fail To Guard Your Own Life,
You Are Like A City Without Walls** (read Proverbs
25:28).

    7. **Failure Occurs When The Wrong
Person Gets Too Close** (see Judges 16:4-21).

    *Treasure The Golden Wall Of Protection God Is
Building Around Your Life.*

    Remember: *Four Kinds Of People Will Be Used
To Distract You From Your Life Assignment.*

18 Wisdom Keys About Focus Every Uncommon Father Should Know

Right Relationships Protect Your Focus.

1. Focus Is Anything That Consumes Your Time, Energy, Finances And Attention.

2. Your Assignment Will Require Your Total Focus. *The Only Reason Men Fail Is Broken Focus.*

While traveling around the world for more than thirty years and speaking more than 14,000 times, I have listened to the details of personal battle conflicts of many hurting people.

3. Satan's Main Goal Is To Simply Break Your Focus Off Your Assignment. When he does this he has mastered you. When he breaks your focus off your Assignment, he has brought pain to the heart of God, Who is his only true enemy.

4. Jesus Encouraged His Disciples To Keep Their Focus On The Kingdom Of God. He assured them that their financial provisions and everything they needed would be produced through absolute *focus upon Him.* "But seek ye first the kingdom of God, and His righteousness; and all these things shall be added unto you" (Matthew 6:33).

5. God Was Fierce In Warning About Distracting Relationships. Listen to the words of God concerning those who would tempt His people to go to another god. "If thy brother, the son of thy mother, or thy son, or thy daughter, or the wife of thy bosom, or thy friend, which is as thine own soul, entice thee secretly, saying, Let us go and serve other gods, which thou hast not known, thou, nor thy fathers; Namely, of the gods of the people which are round about you, nigh unto thee, or far off from thee, from the one end of the earth even unto the other end of the earth; Thou shalt not consent unto him, nor hearken unto him; neither shall thine eye pity him, neither shalt thou spare, neither shalt thou conceal him: But thou shalt surely kill him; thine hand shall be first upon him to put him to death, and afterwards the hand of all the people. And thou shalt stone him with stones, that he die; because he hath sought to thrust thee away from the Lord thy God, which brought thee out of the land of Egypt, from the house of bondage" (Deuteronomy 13:6-10).

   6.   Jesus Addressed Broken Focus In The New Testament. "And if thy right eye offend thee, pluck it out, and cast it from thee: for it is profitable for thee that one of thy members should perish, and not that thy whole body should be cast into hell. And if thy right hand offend thee, cut it off, and cast it from thee: for it is profitable for thee that one of thy members should perish, and not that thy whole body should be cast into hell" (Matthew 5:29,30).

   How do you destroy someone's goal? Give him another one. How do you destroy a dream in someone? Give him another dream. It *fragments his focus*. It *dilutes his energy*.

   7.   Focus Determines Mastery. *Anything that has the ability to keep your attention has mastered you.* Any significant progress toward the completion of your Assignment will require your every thought, every cent, every hour of your life.

   8.   Your Focus Determines Your Energy. Think for a moment. Let us say you are sleepy, laid back on your pillows. The television is on. Suddenly, the telephone rings. Someone in your family has just had a crisis. They are being rushed to the hospital. Do you go back to sleep easily? Of course not. Your focus has changed. Suddenly, you have leaped to your feet. You put on your clothes, jump in your car and head down to the hospital. *Focus* determines your *energy*.

9. What You Look At The Longest Becomes The Strongest In Your Life. The Apostle Paul focused on his future. "Brethren, I count not myself to have apprehended: but this one thing I do, forgetting those things which are behind, and reaching forth unto those things which are before, I press toward the mark for the prize of the high calling of God in Christ Jesus" (Philippians 3:13,14).

10. Broken Focus Creates Insecurity And Instability In Everything Around You. "A double minded man is unstable in all his ways" (James 1:8).

11. Only Focused Faith Can Produce Miracles From The Hand Of God. "But let him ask in faith, nothing wavering. For he that wavereth is like a wave of the sea driven with the wind and tossed. For let not that man think that he shall receive any thing of the Lord" (James 1:6,7).

12. Sight Affects Desire. What you keep looking upon, you eventually pursue. "Mine eye affecteth mine heart because of all the daughters of my city" (Lamentations 3:51). Joshua the remarkable leader of the Israelites, wrote this instruction from God. "Only be thou strong and very courageous, that thou mayest observe to do according to all the law, which Moses My servant commanded thee: turn not

Anything That Keeps
Your Attention
Has Mastered You.

-MIKE MURDOCK

from it to the right hand or to the left, that thou mayest prosper whithersoever thou goest. This book of the law shall not depart out of thy mouth; but thou shalt meditate therein day and night, that thou mayest observe to do according to all that is written therein: for then thou shalt make thy way prosperous, and then thou shalt have good success" (Joshua 1:7,8).

13. Focusing On The Word Of God Daily Is Necessary To Complete Your Assignment Properly. God instructed the people of Israel to teach, train and mentor their children on His words. Listen to this incredible instruction: "Therefore shall ye lay up these My words in your heart and in your soul, and bind them for a sign upon your hand, that they may be as frontlets between your eyes. And ye shall teach them your children, speaking of them when thou sittest in thine house, and when thou walkest by the way, when thou liest down, and when thou risest up. And thou shalt write them upon the door posts of thine house, and upon thy gates:" (Deuteronomy 11:18-20).

14. Focusing, Hearing And Speaking The Word Of God Continually Make You Invincible. "There shall no man be able to stand before you: for the Lord your God shall lay the fear of you and the dread of you upon all the land that ye shall tread upon, as He hath said unto you" (Deuteronomy 11:25). This is one of the reasons I keep cassettes of the Word of God in every room of my home. The first thing I do daily is turn on my tape player and listen to Scriptures being read. It washes my mind, purges my heart and harnesses my focus.

15. Focus Has Reward. "That your days may

be multiplied, and the days of your children, in the land which the Lord sware unto your fathers to give them, as the days of heaven upon the earth. For if ye shall diligently keep all these commandments which I command you, to do them, to love the Lord your God, to walk in all His ways, and to cleave unto Him; Then will the Lord drive out all these nations from before you, and ye shall possess greater nations and mightier than yourselves. Every place whereon the soles of your feet shall tread shall be yours: from the wilderness and Lebanon, from the river, the river Euphrates, even unto the uttermost sea shall your coast be" (Deuteronomy 11:21-24).

16. What You Keep Seeing Determines Your Focus. "I will set no wicked thing before mine eyes: I hate the work of them that turn aside; it shall not cleave to me" (Psalm 101:3).

17. Your Enemy Is Anyone Who Breaks Your Focus From A God-Given Assignment.

18. Your Friend Is Anyone Who Helps Keep You Focused On The Instructions Of God For Your Life.

6 Keys To Protecting Your Focus

1. Recognize That Broken Focus Destroys Your Dreams. It creates an unending parade of tragedies and disasters in your life.

2. Take Personal Responsibility. Be the gatekeeper for your eyes, ears and heart. Nobody else can fully protect you. You must be protected by God, as you yield yourself to Him.

3. Control The Music And Teaching That Enter Your Ears. What You Hear Determines What

You Feel. "And all Israel shall hear, and fear, and shall do no more any such wickedness as this is among you" (Deuteronomy 13:11). What You Hear Determines What You Fear.

4. Keep Continuous Praise On Your Lips And Throughout Your Home. I keep music playing on my property and in my home. Every room in my house has sound and every minute there is music to the Holy Spirit being sung and played. I have speakers on the trees in my seven acre yard. I am determined to protect my focus.

5. Starve Wrong Friendships. Wrong friends do not feed, fuel and fertilize your total focus on your Assignment. Let those friendships die. Samson did not have to date everyone to get his hair cut. He only required one wrong person to destroy his future.

6. Pursue And Permit Only Relationships That Increase Your Focus On Your Assignment. It was late one night in southern Florida. The service had ended. Several preachers wanted to go to a restaurant. As I sat there, I listened to the conversation. (I have two major interests in my life: learning and teaching. Both must take place continually for me to have pleasure!) I listened as everyone discussed ball games, politics and tragedies.

I kept listening for worthy Wisdom Keys that might be imparted; I listened for important questions that might be asked. Neither took place. Several times I attempted to change the direction of the conversation, but it seemed ignored. I was too tired to dominate and take charge, too weary to force the conversation in an appropriate direction.

The Holy Spirit was *not* the focus.

So, I quietly stood and said, "I must leave. God bless each of you." I left. I wish I could have that kind of courage every *year* of my lifetime, every *day* of my lifetime!

6 Important Keys When Someone Threatens To Break Your Focus From Your Assignment

1.   **Remember That God's Assignment For Your Life Is Permanent And Cannot Be Altered By Those Who Do Not Understand You.**

2.   **Spend More Time In The Secret Place Hearing From The Holy Spirit Than You Do Sitting At The Tables Of Others, Hearing Their Insults And Opinions.**

3.   **Remember The Inner Dream God Has Burned Into Your Spirit.** Joseph did this, and he saw the big picture of God throughout his tragedies.

4.   **Reach For Intercessors Who Are Godly, Mature And Compassionate.** "Again I say unto you, That if two of you shall agree on earth as touching any thing that they shall ask, it shall be done for them of My Father which is in heaven" (Matthew 18:19).

5.   **Withdraw From Wrong People.** Remember Samson, who was blinded because he permitted the wrong person to get too close to him? It only takes one person to destroy your Assignment.

6.   **Absorb The Continuous Flow Of Wisdom At The Feet Of Your God-Given Mentor.**

"He that walketh with wise men shall be wise: but a companion of fools shall be destroyed" (Proverbs 13:20). *You can lose in one day what took you twenty years to build.* Do not risk it. *Fight Any Battle Necessary To Maintain Your Focus.*

Remember: *People Will Be Assigned By Hell To Distract, Delay And Derail Your Assignment.*

The Uncommon Father is relentless in his focus, ferocious in protecting the environment of his Family.

He is Uncommon.

DECISION

Will You Accept Jesus As Your Personal Savior Today?

The Bible says, "That if thou shalt confess with thy mouth the Lord Jesus, and shalt believe in thine heart that God hath raised Him from the dead, thou shalt be saved" (Romans 10:9).

Pray this prayer from your heart today!

"Dear Jesus, I believe that You died for me and rose again on the third day. I confess I am a sinner...I need Your love and forgiveness...Come into my heart. Forgive my sins. I receive Your eternal life. Confirm Your love by giving me peace, joy and supernatural love for others. Amen."

☐ Yes, Mike! I made a decision to accept Christ as my personal Savior today. Please send me my free gift of your book, *"31 Keys to a New Beginning"* to help me with my new life in Christ. *(B-48)*

NAME   BIRTHDAY

ADDRESS

CITY   STATE   ZIP

PHONE   E-MAIL

Mail form to:

The Wisdom Center · *4051 Denton Hwy.* · *Ft. Worth, TX 76117*
1-888-WISDOM-1 (1-888-947-3661) · *Website:* ***TheWisdomCenter.tv***

Unless otherwise indicated, all Scripture quotations are taken from the King James Version of the Bible.
The Uncommon Father · ISBN 1-56394-135-X/B-131
Copyright © 2003 by **MIKE MURDOCK**
All publishing rights belong exclusively to Wisdom International
Publisher/Editor: Deborah Murdock Johnson
Published by The Wisdom Center · 4051 Denton Hwy. · Ft. Worth, TX 76117
1-888-WISDOM-1 (1-888-947-3661) · **Website: TheWisdomCenter.tv**
1004◊

DR. MIKE MURDOCK

Has embraced his Assignment to Pursue...Proclaim...and Publish the Wisdom of God to help people achieve their dreams and goals.

Began full-time evangelism at the age of 19, which has continued since 1966.

Has traveled and spoken to more than 14,000 audiences in 38 countries, including East and West Africa, the Orient and Europe.

Noted author of 160 books, including best sellers, "Wisdom For Winning," "Dream Seeds" and "The Double Diamond Principle."

Created the popular "Topical Bible" series for Businessmen, Mothers, Fathers, Teenagers; "The One-Minute Pocket Bible" series, and "The Uncommon Life" series.

Has composed more than 5,700 songs such as "I Am Blessed," "You Can Make It," "God Rides On Wings Of Love" and "Jesus, Just The Mention Of Your Name," recorded by many gospel artists.

Is the Founder of The Wisdom Center, in Fort Worth, Texas.

Has a weekly television program called *"Wisdom Keys With Mike Murdock."*

Has appeared often on TBN, CBN, BET and other television network programs.

Is a Founding Trustee on the Board of International Charismatic Bible Ministries with Oral Roberts.

Has had more than 3,500 accept the call into full-time ministry under his ministry.

THE MINISTRY

1 **Wisdom Books & Literature** - Over 160 best-selling Wisdom Books and 70 Teaching Tape Series.

2 **Church Crusades** - Multitudes are ministered to in crusades and seminars throughout America in "The Uncommon Wisdom Conferences." Known as a man who loves pastors he has focused on church crusades for 38 years.

3 **Music Ministry** - Millions have been blessed by the anointed song writing and singing of Mike Murdock, who has made over 15 music albums and CDs available.

4 **Television** - *"Wisdom Keys With Mike Murdock,"* a nationally-syndicated weekly television program.

5 **The Wisdom Center** - The Ministry Offices of The Mike Murdock Evangelistic Association where Schools of Wisdom have been held.

6 **Schools of the Holy Spirit** - Mike Murdock hosts Schools of the Holy Spirit in many churches to mentor believers on the Person and Companionship of the Holy Spirit.

7 **Schools of Wisdom** - In many major cities Mike Murdock hosts Schools of Wisdom for those who want personalized and advanced training for achieving "The Uncommon Life."

8 **Missions Outreach** - Dr. Mike Murdock's overseas outreaches to 38 countries have included crusades in East and West Africa, South America, the Orient and Europe.

GIFTS OF WISDOM...

FOR *Fathers* ONLY!

▶ **The Businessman's Topical Bible** (B-33 / $10)

▶ **The Father's Topical Bible** (B-35 / $10)

▶ **One-Minute Pocket Bible for Fathers** (B-51 / $5)

▶ **The Uncommon Father** (B-131 / $10)

▶ **The Gift of Wisdom for Fathers** (B-77 / $10)

The Wisdom Center

**WISDOM...
The Greatest
Gift Of All!**

Wisdom Is The Principal Thing

Add 10% For S/H

 4051 Denton Highway • Fort Worth, TX 76117 **1-888-WISDOM1
(1-888-947-3661)** — Website: — THEWISDOMCENTER.TV

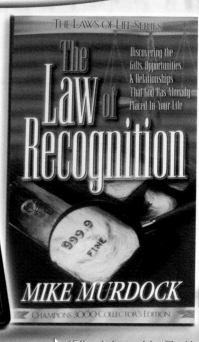

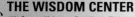

Financial Success.

VIDEO

31 REAON PEOPLE DO NOT RECEIVE THEIR FINANCIAL HARVE$T

MIKE MURDOCK

VIDEO

7 KEYS to 1000 TIMES MORE

The Lord God Of Your Fathers Make You A Thousand Times So Many More As You Are, And Bless You, As He Hath Promised You!
Deuteronomy 1:11

MIKE MURDOCK

▶ 8 Scriptural Reasons You Should Pursue Financial Prosperity

▶ The Secret Prayer Key You Need When Making A Financial Request To God

▶ The Weapon Of Expectation And The 5 Miracles It Unlocks

▶ How To Discern Those Who Qualify To Receive Your Financial Assistance

▶ How To Predict The Miracle Moment God Will Schedule Your Financial Breakthrough

▶ Habits Of Uncommon Achievers

▶ The Greatest Success Law I Ever Discovered

▶ How To Discern Your Place Of Assignment, The Only Place Financial Provision Is Guaranteed

▶ 3 Secret Keys In Solving Problems For Others

The Wisdom Center

Video Pak AMVIDEO | **$30**
Buy 1-Get 1 Free
(A $60 Value!)

Wisdom Is The Principal Thing

Add 10% For S/H

Songs From The Secret Place

The Music Ministry of MIKE MURDOCK

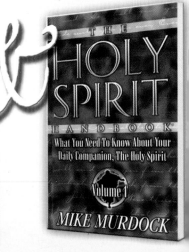

Love Songs To The Holy Spirit Birthed In The Secret Place

The Wisdom Center

6 Tapes | $30

PAK-007

Wisdom Is The Principal Thing

Free B
B-100 ($10

ENCLOSED

Wisdom Is The Principa

Songs...

1. A Holy Place
2. Anything You Want
3. Everything Comes From You
4. Fill This Place With Your Presence
5. First Thing Every Morning
6. Holy Spirit, I Want To Hear You
7. Holy Spirit, Move Again
8. Holy Spirit, You Are Enough
9. I Don't Know What I Would Do Without You
10. I Let Go (Of Anything That Stops Me)
11. I'll Just Fall On You
12. I Love You, Holy Spirit
13. I'm Building My Life Around You
14. I'm Giving Myself To You
15. I'm In Love! I'm In Love!
16. I Need Water (Holy Spirit, You're My Well)
17. In The Secret Place
18. In Your Presence, I'm Always Changed
19. In Your Presence (Miracles Are Born)
20. I've Got To Live In Your Presence
21. I Want To Hear Your Voice
22. I Will Do Things Your Way
23. Just One Day At A Time
24. Meet Me In The Secret Place
25. More Than Ever Before
26. Nobody Else Does What You Do
27. No No Walls!
28. Nothing Else Matters Anymore (Since I've Been In The Presence Of You Lord)
29. Nowhere Else
30. Once Again You've Answered
31. Only A Fool Would Try (To Live Without You)
32. Take Me Now
33. Teach Me How To Please You
34. There's No Place I'd Rather Be
35. Thy Word Is All That Matters
36. When I Get In Your Presence
37. You're The Best Thing (That's Ever Happened To Me)
38. You Are Wonderful
39. You've Done It Once
40. You Keep Changing Me
41. You Satisfy

Add 10% For S/H

The Uncommon Woman

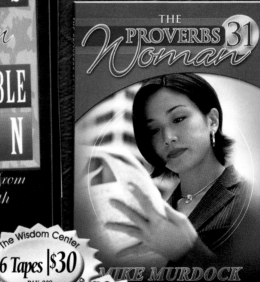

- ▸ Master Keys In Understanding The Man In Your Life
- ▸ The One Thing Every Man Attempts To Move Away From
- ▸ The Dominant Difference Between A Wrong Woman And A Right Woman
- ▸ What Causes Men To Withdraw

MIKE MURDOCK

THE WISDOM FOR WOMEN SERIES

THIRTY - ONE SECRETS of an UNFORGETTABLE WOMAN

Master Secrets from the Life of Ruth

THE WISDOM CENTER
MURDOCK•P.O. Box 99• Denton, Texas

THE WISDOM CENTER
MIKE MURDOCK•P.O. Box 99• Denton, Texas

31 Secrets of an Unforgettable Woman

The Wisdom Center
6 Tapes | $30
PAK-009
Wisdom Is The Principal Thing

Free Book Enclosed!
Wisdom Is The Principal Thing

MIKE MURDOCK
MENTORSHIP PROGRAM OF WISDOM

Add 10% For S/H

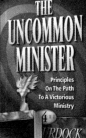

GIFTS OF WISDOM...

FOR *Fathers* ONLY!

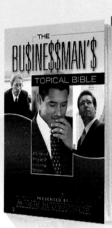

- ▶ **The Businessman's Topical Bible** (B-33 / $10)
- ▶ **The Father's Topical Bible** (B-35 / $10)
- ▶ **One-Minute Pocket Bible for Fathers** (B-51 / $5)
- ▶ **The Uncommon Father** (B-131 / $10)
- ▶ **The Gift of Wisdom for Fathers** (B-77 / $10)

The Wisdom Center

**WISDOM...
The Greatest
Gift Of All!**

Wisdom Is The Principal Thing

Add 10% For S/H

 THE WISDOM CENTER
4051 Denton Highway • Fort Worth, TX 76117

**1-888-WISDOM1
(1-888-947-3661)**

Website:
THEWISDOMCENTER.TV

H

GIFTS OF WISDOM...

SPECIALTY *Bibles*

*Each Book Sold Separately

- ▶ **The Businessman's Topical Bible** (B-33 / $10)
- ▶ **The Children's Topical Bible** (B-154 / $10)
- ▶ **The Father's Topical Bible** (B-35 / $10)
- ▶ **The Grandparent's Topical Bible** (B-34 / $10)
- ▶ **The Minister's Topical Bible** (B-32 / $10)
- ▶ **The Mother's Topical Bible** (B-36 / $10)
- ▶ **The New Believer's Topical Bible** (B-37 / $10)
- ▶ **The Seeds of Wisdom Topical Bible** (B-31 / $10)
- ▶ **The ServiceMan's Topical Bible** (B-138 / $10)

- ▶ **The Teen's Topical Bible** (B-30 / $10)
- ▶ **The Traveler's Topical Bible** (B-139 / $10)
- ▶ **The Widow's Topical Bible** (B-38 / $10)

The Wisdom Center

Only $10 each

Wisdom Is The Principal Thing

Add 10% For S/H

J **THE WISDOM CENTER**
4051 Denton Highway • Fort Worth, TX 76117

1-888-WISDOM1
(1-888-947-3661)

Website:
THEWISDOMCENTER.TV

My Gift Of Appreciation...
The Wisdom Commentary

The Wisdom Commentary includes 52 topics...for mentoring your family every week of the year.

These topics include:

- Abilities
- Achievement
- Anointing
- Assignment
- Bitterness
- Blessing
- Career
- Change
- Children
- Dating
- Depression
- Discipline
- Divorce
- Dreams And Goals
- Enemy
- Enthusiasm
- Favor
- Finances
- Fools

- Giving
- Goal-Setting
- God
- Happiness
- Holy Spirit
- Ideas
- Intercession
- Jobs
- Loneliness
- Love
- Mentorship
- Ministers
- Miracles
- Mistakes
- Money
- Negotiation
- Prayer
- Problem-Solving
- Protégés

- Satan
- Secret Place
- Seed-Faith
- Self-Confidence
- Struggle
- Success
- Time-Management
- Understanding
- Victory
- Weaknesses
- Wisdom
- Word Of God
- Words
- Work

THE *Mike Murdock* COLLECTOR'S EDITION

The Wisdom Commentary of MIKE MURDOCK

THE **Wisdom Commentary 1**

VOL. 1

B-136

Gift Of Appreciation
For Your Sponsorship Seed of $100 or More
Gift Of Appreciation

y Gift Of Appreciation To My Sponsors!
hose Who Sponsor One Square Foot In
e Completion Of The Wisdom Center!

nk you so much for becoming a part of this wonderful project...The completion of The Wisdom Center! total purchase and renovation cost of this facility (10,000 square feet) is just over $1,000,000. This is oximately $100 per square foot. **The Wisdom Commentary is my Gift of Appreciation for your nsorship Seed of $100...that sponsors one square foot of The Wisdom Center. Become a Sponsor!** will love this Volume 1, of The Wisdom Commentary. It is my exclusive Gift of Appreciation for The dom Key Family who partners with me in the Work of God as a Sponsor.

Add 10% For S/H

 THE WISDOM CENTER 4051 Denton Highway • Fort Worth, TX 76117 **1-888-WISDOM1 (1-888-947-3661)** Website: THEWISDOMCENTER.TV **K**

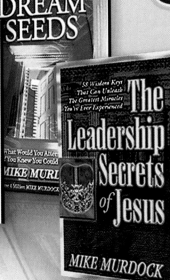
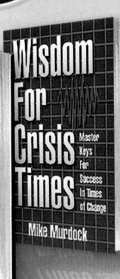

The Wisdom Journal

"Write The Things Which Thou Hast Seen, And The Things Which Are, And The Things Which Shall Be Hereafter."

-Revelation 1:19

My Wisdom Journal

Stunningly beautiful deep Black and Gold Leatherette. Contains 160 pages for your personal journalizing and diary...a different Wisdom Key for each day...it also includes:

- ► 101 Wisdom Keys
- ► 31 Facts About Favor
- ► 31 Facts About Wisdom
- ► 31 Facts About The Holy Spirit
- ► 31 Qualities Of An Unforgettable Woman
- ► 58 Leadership Secrets Of Jesus
- ► Read The Bible Through In A Year Program
- ► Sample Page For Effective Note Taking

The Wisdom Center

$20 Each

B-163

Wisdom Is The Principal Thing

Add 10% For S/H

  THE WISDOM CENTER 4051 Denton Highway • Fort Worth, TX 76117 **1-888-WISDOM1** **(1-888-947-3661)** Website: **THEWISDOMCENTER.TV**

JOIN THE
Wisdom Key 3000
TODAY!

Dear Partner,

God has connected us!

I have asked the Holy Spirit for 3000 Special Partners who will plant a monthly Seed of $58.00 to help me bring the gospel around the world. (58 represents 58 kinds of blessing in the Bible.)

Will you become my monthly Faith Partner in The Wisdom Key 3000? Your monthly Seed of $58.00 is so powerful in helping heal broken lives. When you sow into the work of God, 4 Miracle Harvests are guaranteed in Scripture:

► Uncommon Protection (Mal. 3:10,11)
► Uncommon Favor (Lk. 6:38)
► Uncommon Health (Isa. 58:8)
► Financial Ideas and Wisdom (Deut. 8:18)

Your Faith Partner,

Mike Murdock

□ **Yes Mike, I want to join The Wisdom Key 3000. Enclosed is my monthly Seed-Faith Promise of □ $58 □ Other $_____. Please rush The Wisdom Key Partnership Pak to me today!**

□ CHECK   □ MONEY ORDER   □ AMEX   □ DISCOVER   □ MASTERCARD   □ VISA

Credit Card # _____ Exp. ___/___

Signature _____

Name _____ Birth Date ___/___/___

Address _____

City _____ State _____ Zip _____

Phone _____ E-Mail _____

Seed-Faith offerings are used to support the Mike Murdock Evangelistic Association, The Wisdom Center and all its programs. Ministry reserves the right to redirect funds as needed in order to carry out our charitable purpose.   Add 10% For S/H

Clip and mail completed form to:

THE WISDOM CENTER   **1-888-WISDOM1**   Website:
P.O. Box 99, Denton, Texas 76202   **(1-888-947-3661)**   WWW.THEWISDOMCENTER.TV   **0**

UNCOMMON WISDOM FOR UNCOMMON ACHIEVERS

Dream 7 PAK

► **The Leadership Secrets Of Jesus** (B-91 / $10)

► **Dream Seeds** (B-11 / $9)

► **Secrets Of The Richest Man Who Ever Lived** (B-99 / $10)

► **The Assignment; The Dream And The Destiny, Volume 1** (B-74 / $10)

► **The Holy Spirit Handbook** (B-100 / $10)

► **The Law Of Recognition** (B-114 / $10)

► **31 Reasons People Do Not Receive Their Financial Harvest** (B-82 / $12)

The Wisdom Center

7 Books for only

$50 *$71 Value*

WBL-23

Wisdom Is The Principal Thing

Add 10% For S/H

THE WISDOM CENTER
4051 Denton Highway • Fort Worth, TX 76117

1-888-WISDOM1
(1-888-947-3661)

Website:
THEWISDOMCENTER.TV